T I D

F U R T H E S

R E A C H

****

More Seaside Poetry

2023 - 2025

G o d f r e y   H o l m e s

Godfrey H Holmes

March 2025

Tide's Furthest Reach:

More Seaside Poetry : 2023 to 2025

****

ISBN : 978-0-9934644-5-4

****

NETHERMOOR BOOKS
"St. Elphin"
12 North Promenade, Withernsea HU19 2DP
Telephone : 01964-615258

Contact the Author godfrey.holmes@btinternet.com

****

Whilst all the proceeds from the sale of this book go to
<< The Friends of St. Nicholas' Withernsea >>
the Author's Viewpoint &
Choice of Content is his - & his alone.

****

Dedicated to
Darrin & Flo' Stevens,
Russell & Christine
Mathers :
who at every opportunity
keep the Ship afloat...

CONTENTS :

****

INTRODUCTION

My three previous books of Collected Poetry:

<<*Beside the Great North Sea*>> (2012)
<<*Sandcastles Do Not Fall*>> (2013) &
<<*As Shadows Lengthen*>> (2023)

were all inspired by the Seaside in general, my Retirement to Withernsea – in singular competition to be *the unknown Seaside Resort of England* – in particular.

This does not mean a whole pile of Poems about seagulls, beaches, and deckchairs! I do stray, often, into the fields of human nature, the absurdity of everyday life, and "life's little ironies."

And for someone like myself with a sometimes wry sense of humour, time and tide do indeed go together. I relish in the obscure; in snippets of news soon forgotten by alternative observers.

Of course, there is some risk in *topographical Poetry*, Verse anchored in place: that certain Readers who know nothing of that *geography* will miss the usual photography, the received imagery of mind and memory. By way of contrast, Poems drawn from the streets of London or Edinburgh - or even Oxford - can draw freely on a well of Reader familiarity.

So although the Content of "*Tide's Furthest Reach*" is not much different from its three predecessors, particular East Riding of Yorkshire places are mentioned more often. This time, indicatively, my selection draws on a whole series of

Poems submitted to *The Holderness Gazette* for its weekly *Poetry Platform*. These over a number of months during 2023 and 2024, with very few weeks went missing. For that fantastic exposure, many thanks to Editor Sam Hawcroft

That discipline explains the *Urgency* to this book. Had anything happened in the past week: *not normally Political,* but writeable-aboutable? Or had I spotted something unusual on the pavement – or from the alternative warmest or coldest seat on the top-deck of a, *by me frequently patronized*, Number 75 Bus to, or and from, Kingston-upon-Hull?

I'll never know quite what gives me the inspiration nor the ability - *inability?* - to relate often humdrum events in different metres; different rhymes (or *the absence* of rhyme); different lengths of individual stanza.

I've never been a fan of radical revision: this not a sign of laziness, more a fear of straining both text and impact. Yes it would be possible now, *and* at the moment of composition, to alter the original; indeed to *improve* the original text(s). But that always risks a half-bake, or an over-bake. I do, of course, still have an obligation to correct factual inaccuracies, mis-spellings, also accidental identification of persons maybe not always shown in their best light.

In conclusion, many of my most recent Poems, Stories, reproduced here are rather raw, unexplained, even inexplicable. As such, they achieve what all Verse should: to leave the Reader wanting more.

Godfrey Holmes, St. Elphin, January 2025

<u>Introduction to Poem Number. One:</u>

By coincidence, my third book of Poems: << As Shadows Lengthen>> *was dedicated to, and sold entirely for, Withernsea's imaginative Pier Project, masterminded by the then entirely voluntary: Withernsea Pier and Promenade Association.*

In common with many other Withernsea residents I was crestfallen, and stopped in my tracks, by this remarkable Project's sinking forever.

The Poem "A Pier Without Peer" *unusually wrote itself, once I had internalized the very distinctive Hymn tune :* " God is Working His Purpose Out." *Even when I'm composing stanzas not the least bit religious, I do rely on some very accessible Hymn or Song tunes, never more than for:* "The Night of her Rescue," *written specially to showcase:* <<Sandcastles Do Not Fall>>.

****

ONE) **A PIER WITHOUT PEER**

Our Pier was working its purpose out
As year succeeded year;
Our Pier was working its purpose out
And the time was drawing near:
Nearer and nearer drew the time:
The time that should surely be
When wild waves would lap round piles sunk in sand,
As day-trippers strode out to Sea .
Many the plans for planners drawn:

Fresh from the drawing-board;
Many the plans for planners drawn:
As much as found funds could afford.
"Give ear to our scheme ye Councillors!
Look far beyond Twin Towers!
And see our Resort with attraction bestowed-
Fruit borne of your diverse powers."

Scouts went to Cleethorpes, then to Ryde;
To Bournemouth and to Deal:
Saw how these Towns had built their Piers
From a fountain of Goodwill.
Yet objections were hoarse and our Pier rammed off course:
No heed giv'n to Withernsea's pride;
Ten thousand hours on a dream down the drain:
Brighter future by stealth denied.

Introduction to Poem Number Two:

In common with a number of other swimmers never seen further out to Sea than 80 yards, I listen to the BBC's Shipping Forecast as frequently as possible. Skilled meteorologists speak its warnings in dulcet tones: accidental Poetry.

On the other hand, normal weather forecasts come across as prosaic: exciting only when something is about to go wrong! Most days, the rest of the country is going to have splendid sunshine, & very little precipitation: the East Yorkshire Coast a notable exception!

TWO) **EXCEPT FOR HUMBER**

" Phew! What a Scorcher!"
Examinations: utter torture!
Sunshine hours without number -
".....except for Humber."

"Hottest-day-of-the-Year!"
Men in shorts may now appear!
Salads of Quiche & cool cucumber-
".....except for Humber."

"Families are flocking to the Coast..."
Ramblers on hillsides sure to roast!
See day-trippers with all their lumber -
".....except for Humber."

" People bathing in the Ocean!"
Cleaning upstairs but a notion?
At eventide: perspiring slumber -
".....except for Humber."

" Why is East Yorkshire always excepted?
Bands of thick cloud so widely expected?"
North-East winds bringing skies so dull -
".....*including Hull*! "

Introduction to Poem Number Three:

In a sometimes vain attempt to attract more Tourists, several Towns & Cities have resorted to Treasure Trails: these not to gather clues or money or Easter Eggs, less so to read literature tied to lamp-posts.

No: the modern Trail relies on huge acrylic Butterflies or Soldiers or Elephants or Frogs. So as not to miss out, one particular Winter the East Riding of Yorkshire commissioned a series of giant Puffins (always a popular even if elusive sea-bird, unlike the widely sanctioned herring-gull!).

Therefore one morning, Withernsea woke up to 3-foot-6 high acrylic Puffins. And very well crafted they were, each at a cost of several hundred pounds. One fine sculpture was stolen straightway. Two or three other Puffins stayed on the Promenade; next to the Lifeboat Station too, giving great pleasure to any number of passers-by who photographed them......

****

THREE) **FLIGHT of the PUFFINS**

Our Puffins are missing
Moreover, I am missing them!
Nor knowing where, exactly, they have landed?
Puffin Waxholme; Puffin Promenade;
Puffin Lifeboat:
All have flown away

Flying to some far-flung Harbour?
Now seated next to other Puffins
From other Strands.
And while these Puffins -
These amazing Puffins -
Sojourned in this Resort:
How comforting, how reassuring, their Presence!
So beautiful, so comical, so colourful their Creation:
Each resplendent in his different outfit!

But now they have gone to feed on eels
Alongside equally distinctive seals?
Fleeing, I feel, I dread
So far away from what has been their home:
Perched as they were overlooking our Ocean, *their Ocean*:
At Waxholme, on Promenade, gracing the Lifeboat....
Only never to return?

Introduction to Poem Number Four:

"Down Central Promenade" is very much an Insider Poem: reliant as it is on some local knowledge of Withernsea, Yorkshire's Southernmost Seaside Resort.

However I include it here because it illustrates vast changes in Tourist footfall since the Trains stopped running on October 19th., 1964. On some old maps Central Promenade is named, or confused with, Queen's Promenade. I keep with "Central" because this stretch of traffic-free paving lies between North & South

Promenades: its crowning glory the iconic Pier Towers imaginatively imitating the architecture of North Wales' Conwy Castle.

****

FOUR) **DOWN CENTRAL PROMENADE....**

When we're completely ready, let me tell you the tale of "Teddys" :
Beginning at Pier Towers, avoiding some April Showers,
We'll head South towards Spurn, while sea-ward our eyes will turn:
To our Left a rampart strong - where a building did once belong:
A Night-Club well-frequented; by some folks hotly resented...
By no means a building beautiful: on fire alerting M.P. dutiful;
Tons of concrete once its foundation; rocks of granite stopping inundation:
A whole promontory once so visible; as "Sun Terrace" verging on risible;
For Health & Safety a Site soon fenced: chains of ply-board a task immense;
Frail panels first painted yellow attracting a certain imaginative fellow.
Soon these boards with photos were covered: With's hist'ry by walkers discovered;
Until ply-wood's life expired: promenaders no longer inspired.
"Should this Site be bought for a bounty?" was the puzzle presented to County....
Instead choosing low iron railings: disguising all previous failings.

Introduction to Poem Number Five:

Twice a Year, Withernsea's Central Promenade hosts a spectacular Procession of Tractors: 40 or more, of all makes and sizes. Into the Resort they trundle down Seaside Road at about Midday one Sunday; park up for an hour; then return – again in orderly Procession- down Pier Road towards whichever agricultural Village they had all started off from.....

This is the Holderness farming community showing off their work-horses ancient & modern: machines normally kept in barns , or garages. So antique are some of these Tractors that they are no longer in production; no longer seen working in the very fields, acres of very fertile fields, where crops such as rye, wheat, barley, potatoes, rape, sunflowers are grown.

Now you would think Withernsea already has enough Tractors: available each day to haul as many as seven fishing boats or seven private boats across the sands towards full tide, and back. Because Withernsea, Hornsea, Easington and Tunstall have no formal harbours. Fishing boats actually ask *to be beached, their Tractors fitted with exhausts positioned at seat level to keep the Ocean out!*

Here I am inspired by my 1st. witnessed Procession – every penny collected, for Marie Curie or an alternative Charity. Brilliant!

****

FIVE) **BIG WHEELS TO FOLLOW ? 2013-2023**

(*A Poet's Imagination in Overdrive*)

Camilla stops by With on a Tractor,
How do those Crowds distract her!
She came to Town on a Tractor.

Prince Charles reaches With on a Fergie:
Before the dreaded lurgi....
He entered Town on a Fergie.

The Queen's Golden Coach is a Farmall:
Aware of her Crowning's charm-all!
She rides down the Mall on a Farmall.

The Duke takes his Throne on a Ford:
His patience now reaping reward!
He glides past Big Ben on a Ford.

Will follows his Dad on a Deere -
This Brother displaying no fear!
Will leaves Buck House on a Deere.

Kate Middleton proceeds on a Massey:
Her Headwear looks so sassy!
The Duchess waves from a Massey!

Introduction to Poem Number Six:

Along with most people born mid-20th. Century, I mourned the insolvency and later the loss of American chain store: F. W. Woolworth – which had presence on most of the High Streets of Britain, including Withernsea's.

In fact, some commentators' definition of a Town was "one big enough to have a Woolworth's."

Times changed and Woolworth's, including Big W. couldn't fit the bill. But amazingly, there were several firms waiting in the wings to sell a little of everything: Wilko, B&M, Home Bargains among them. Admittedly, Wilkinsons followed Woolworth's into the Wilderness, but its erstwhile Competitors are stronger than ever....

****

SIX) **THE BESTEST GENERALIST ?**

"*Top Quality, Low Prices*"
Doesn't sound quite right-
Try: " *High Prices, Low Quality*"?
Sounds no better - as I enter one of Woolworth's worthy successors:
This a "Generalist" Store selling everything from cookies to kiddy's clothes -
Cheapo but not as cheap as "*Stack 'em High, Sell 'em Low*"?
So I'll try again. Possibly borrow from the competition?
"*Top Brands, Bottom Prices*":
But that's still not quite right?

So how about the obvious one:
" *Highest Quality, Lowest Prices*"?
Great! Except that one was patented
By a little Grocer on the busy Trentham Road out of Longton, in 1956...
And written in posh writing across their canvas sun-blinds....
So I'll have one more try:
" *Maximum Choice, Minimum Outlay*"?
" *Highest Reach, Lowest Satisfaction*"?
" *Widest Range, Narrowest Offer*"?
" *Broadest Isles, Titchiest Sails*" ?

These only to prompt my hasty retreat to Customer Service
For what could be the most inspiring of inspirations:
" *Fullest Shelves, Emptiest Purses*" ?
" *Smallest Margins, Biggest Difference*"?
" *Steepest Rises, Deepest Indifference*" ?
Don't blame me! Take it up with the General...

<u>*Introduction to Poem Number Seven:*</u>

A frequent patron of Hull's usually brilliant Truck Theatre, occasionally other Arenas too, I found myself puzzling about other theatre-goers; more other concert-goers who managed to get in buckshee for the second-half of any Performance: this second half rarely subject to an entry check! Success depends on quite a timetabled *half-time break:*

[Arthur a feeble pun for <<Half A>>] .....

****

SEVEN) **ARTHUR**

Let me introduce you to Arthur:
Show-off Arthur, show-stopper Arthur
Arthur C. Little :
Seeing little because he wants to see little;
Coming second because he wants to come in second!
Never first; never at 7-45-
More at 8-55, just after the Interval....
Because Arthur always enters the Auditorium
Just after the Interval - or during the Interval -
To see the rest of the Performance,
Maybe *the best* of the Performance,
But definitely only half a Performance....
And all unassuming, while Arthur is assuming nothing
Because he's done his Homework.
Unassisted by any "better half," he still gets the better half
Free and for nothing:
Half a ticket going spare - but only for the second half.
And, as you would expect, Arthur knows a sell-out
When he sees one - or rather doesn't see one
Because all the tickets have sold out:
One - or rather half of one - to avoid?
Far better to concentrate on the three-quarters of shows,
Three-quarters of operas, three-quarters of plays
Where only three-quarters of the seats have been sold -
Leaving a choice of one quarter of available seats for Arthur
To avail himself of, half of the time -
Because half-a-loafer's better than none...

<u>Introduction to Poem Number Eight :</u>

Like so many people born in the late 1940s, 1950s or 1960s, Queen Elizabeth II sat on the throne for as long as we could remember: decade after decade, jubilee after jubilee. So even the Republicans among us could not imagine where we'd be on the day she'd die? Hoping we should not die before she did...

Would there be two weeks of national mourning? Would everybody wear black? The BBC go off air immediately in case any programme in the pipeline should show a hint of disrespect or disregard?

We half expected the older Duke of Edinburgh – never *called King - to depart this life first, in other words to miss out on his Wife's Platinum. But further details, although practised in Pall Mall late some nights, remained unspoken.*

Shamelessly borrowing the evocative title of a popular Sunday Night TV show: here I bring the late Queen to the flatlands of Holderness....

****

EIGHT) **MONARCH of the GLEN ?**

She was indeed Monarch of the Glen
And that is how - & where -
Our Queen chose - or did not choose ? -
To spend her last days.

Beside still waters;
Entranced by unutterable beauty;
Secluded; Secure
Beneath the ever-shifting skies
Of Balmoral.

But equally our Head-of-State
Might, that momentous day,
Have been in Patrington?
Visiting St. Patrick's Church in all its splendour;
Hovering over the Meridian:

She espying Grimsby's Dock Tower on the distant Horizon;
Able - & willing - to be wheeled along Withernsea's South Promenade.
After Luncheon.

For the wild, windy,
Turbulent, tempestuous, North Sea
Has its own majesty;
Its own very different combination of the elements.
Therefore: in all our imaginations
Noblest Monarch of the Glen,
You are not far removed.....

ΩΩΩΩΩΩΩΩΩΩΩΩΩΩΩΩ

Introduction to Poem Number Nine

My interest in J.C.B. diggers began when a railway train once dropped me at Uttoxeter, their birthplace.

And my later fascination was rekindled when I realized a daily commute passed by its Cousin: a Caterpillar plant.

But what really got me going was the day-by-day demolition of an historic public house ten miles away. This destruction was contemporaneous with the strengthening of Withernsea's North Promenade: an operation where very many J.C.B. diggers had to flee twice a day to avoid the very present threat of expensive immersion in the oncoming tide.

These wonderful machines are so powerful; also so adaptable to whichever job is to hand. Nobody argues with a J.C.B. digger. Yet you rarely see one trundling along a main road without the assistance of a low-loader.

****

NINE) **DON'T YOU SEE J.C.?**

Our Pub is called : *<<The Excavator>>* :
And true to its name
An Excavator sits secure above its main entrance:
Not any old Excavator
Nor a foot-by-foot model of an Excavator -
But a real JCB: *top drawer*

Drawn to the fore for many an excavation,
Many a demolition.

You'd have imagined somebody by now
Would have dismembered this JCB -
And copied it? :
<<Made in Hong Kong>>?
Brought to you courtesy of
The People's Republic of China?

But if industrial espionage goes on -
And undoubtedly industrial espionage
Does go on:
The excavator's chosen Excavator -
And its blood brothers on Site-
Own a very different heritage:
In auction , a very different provenance.

And were the whole sales' pitch
Counter-counterfeit:
There is less chance
Our sturdy JCB digger would be counterfeit -
Now more able to keep track in more than one way -
Boldly transported to developers
As their preferred transport whenever on site.
I'll drink to that!

ΩΩΩΩΩΩΩΩΩΩΩΩΩΩΩΩΩΩ

Introduction to Poem Number Ten :

Trends by definition are trendy: the twists and turns of what is fashionable : principally "followed" on social media. And one such preoccupation, dare, is to add a locked padlock to some beauty-spot or another.

Each padlock the symbol of romance; the acknowledgement of everlasting love. Love cemented, reciprocated, perhaps at that particular beauty-spot.

But one couple's touching gesture is another tourist's, another town planner's, nuisance. Will these padlocks rust and not be renewed. Worse, will these padlocks be supplemented by accessories such as cuddly teddy-bears and mournful greetings' cards? Even worse than that: will padlocks too numerous weigh down the wires meant to protect those same passers-by.

Nonetheless: a fascinating subject for Poetry....

****

TEN) **WEIGHED DOWN?**

Between myself and the river are chains:
A multitude of chains....
And fastened to those chains are padlocks:
So many padlocks each chain droops
Out of sympathy with its fellow chains
Similarly weighed down?
For now not an inch of any chain -

To the Left or the Right -
Is left free, unburdened by padlocked padlocks.

And in turn each of these pendants is different:
Some red, some blue - most of silver or of bronze,
Not a few betraying their age,
Beset by rust and weather less kind
Than those people so kind as to merit commemoration
Through pretend incarceration.

And maybe each festoon, decaying, has a story to tell?
Some yet to be liberated using long-forgotten combinations?
Others elusively set free by the turning of a long-lost key?
A few - just a few - telling each curious onlooker
Name, date-of-birth, date-of-death;
Others trailing - trialing - a Poem, once unhinged?

And does all this clasping – clamping - this grasping of immortality - make sense?
Or has all sense - or sensibility - lapsed long ago?
Here lives lived, lovers loved, mourning mourned: memories
Secret, sacred; outside the comprehension of all outsiders -
And beyond their challenge:
Locks unlockable, beliefs unbelievable, relief irretrievable
Forever.....?

Introduction to Poem Number Eleven :

I had long been interested in Estate Cars: more developed now to encompass Land-Rovers, Range-Rovers, Sports' Utility Vehicles, 4-by-4s, and Chelsea Tractors. One day, whilst waiting in Hedon for the next

Number 75 Bus back to Withernsea, it suddenly dawned on me that most passing, or parked, vehicles were sizeable off-roaders: yet nowhere near the hills and battlefields for which such Jeeps were invented....

****

ELEVEN) **MO-TOWN ?**

Near -far?-away
Stands Port-Town
Mo-Town
Hedon.

Hedon :
Mo-Town
Where wheeler-dealers
Deal in wheels
Many wheels!
The Secret of 4-Wheel Drive!

Land Rovers, Range Rovers,
Highlanders, Outlanders,
XCs, X-3s,
Atecas, Delicas,
Pajeros, Turismos,
Dusters and Foresters,
Shoguns eclipsed by the Eclipse?

4-Wheel Drives:
Hedonistas' Fashion

4-Wheel Drives:
Hedonistas' Passion
4-Wheel Drives:
Hear Hedonistas Boasting
4-Wheel Drives:
See Hedonistas Coasting

Introduction to Poem Number Twelve:

Unbeknown to most of my fellow-travellers or nearby diners, I am an inveterate – and insatiably curious – people watcher.

But the art of Mass Observation is to give no clue whatsoever that you are rubber-necking; worse, that you are eavesdropping!

Most study of persons nearby does not include or depend upon audio. As with the following scenario, no words were or are exchanged. By way of contrast, visibility is of essence, intent visibility.

****

TWELVE) **LORD of the RINGS**

I first notice the rings through his ears and nose:
Three in total: golden, shiny, each the size of a five-pound coin
Though possibly costing more?

Next I see the necklaces round his neck
Bangles encircling his wrists -
Bangles of brass and silver and stainless steel:
Some plain; others, inspired by Celtic mythology, patterned.
And , crossing the adornment of his Right-hand wrist:
Is a bold wrist-watch whose story stays untold,
Its funky face and clunky surround indebted to the New Age.

Yet the more I study the man sitting opposite me
The more complicated the rings adorning his 8 fingers -
Certainly more than 8 in number.
Here the metals, also the precious stones inlaid,
Are too complex, too varied, to describe in a single sentence:
Their essence, extravagance.

Heaven knows how - or when - this gaunt gentleman
Acquired his pretty - and pretty diverse - ornamentation?
Nor what entered his head when entering City jewellery shops
To add to his exceptionally rococo collection of decoration?
Nor is there any indication - yet -
What bangles encircle his hidden *ankles*?
Nor what exotic tattoos the loose-hanging sleeves
Of his loose-fitting sweatshirt *hide* from the outside World?
Sufficient to say, this day, I witness his true colours: unfurled?

ΩΩΩΩΩΩΩΩΩΩΩΩΩΩΩΩ

Introduction to Poem Number Thirteen:

On East Yorkshire's rather cool and blustery coast sun-hats are rarely required – though it is always useful to have one tucked into your beach-bag.

Therefore I was amazed to see how many sun-hats were actually available in Withernsea for purchase, plus a colourful array of buckets and spades....

****

THIRTEEN) : **A HEAD for EVERY HAT?**

And in my dream I see
Three poles, three hat-stands
As if belonging to a previous Milliner:
Yet this no ordinary spinster?
Even though, before Winter, she out to sell hats;
Any hats; many hats, depending:
Circular hats all - and all canvas to the touch;
Distractive hats, attractive hats:
Hats of every hue - and almost every design:
Mine to choose, then use, depending.

Flat caps rather downbeat, down-market,
In the 1920s - but one Century on
These vaguely conical, vaguely comical, caps
Are altogether different from - and not indifferent to Fashion:
Veggie caps, onions, cucumbers, leeks or chillies;
Fruity caps, apples, pears, plums or bananas;

Scary caps, wyverns, werewolves, dybbuks, smurfs;
Fishy caps, dabs, crabs, eels or seals;
Sporty caps, footballs, rugby balls, greyhounds, Lions;
Beatles, butterflies, daisies, ice-scoops; hoops -
Or simple zig-zags, woolly clouds.

And in my dream, I long for the Sun:
Sun strong and bright, just right for wearing
The hat for which I am now reaching, while teaching
Others protection, elementary protection,
Protection from the elements.

ΩΩΩΩΩΩΩΩΩΩΩΩΩΩΩΩΩΩ

Introduction to Poem Number Fourteen:

When I traced among my vinyl Records an "original" Beatles' Sergeant Pepper's Lonely Hearts Band LP, I sought out the type of shop in Hull that might purchase it for a couple of hundred pounds...

The curiosity Record shop I discovered, just 15 minutes' brisk walk from the Railway Station, did not disappoint. But the price did! It turned out my collector's Valhalla was an American copy!

****

FOURTEEN) **BEATING THE RECORD?**

All tech fails -
The true believer wails:
Video-tapes bought less than vapes;
The "Black-berry" less than sherry;
Nokia phones less than drones;
Rubber stamp less than lava-lamp;
Filofax bought less than pac-a-macs;
Kalamazoo less than a horse-shoe;
Games' console up against the insole;
Egg-whisk o'ertaking floppy-disk;
Knit pom-poms, not CD-roms;
Dinky-cars, not S.L.R.

So what chance I to sell
My 45 of "William Tell"?
And who on Earth will buy
My 33 "Fam'ly Stone and Sly"?
Who wants *Records* in Spring Bank?
How will Reeves with The Beatles rank?

Dropping down steps into a cavern.
Is it a shop? - or is it a tavern?
Has this horde got any keeper?
No room left for carpet-sweeper.
Vinyl, vinyl, everywhere:
Nine score Singles' worthy to share.
And tucked away : filmed D.V.D.s -
And stacked EPs...

Down cluttered aisle I squeeze.
One poor owner not needing donors;
Stock, more stock, to price, against the clock.
His heart's desire: the *discerning* buyer:
Does idle chat make me a liar?
Perhaps I've squandered all his time -
And left, amazed, not spending dime?

Introduction to Poem Number Fifteen:

Diners are nothing if not set in their ways. And one of their ways is to want to sit with their spouse, their partner, or their lover alone. *Unencumbered by any sharer(s) of their table. This although they are part of one assured twosome for 364 days till February 14th. next .*

****

FIFTEEN) **A ST.VALENTINE's DINNER FOR ONE**

His Valentine's Dinner booked for One
Has, at seven, only just begun:
One 6-course Menu before him laid;
One bottle of Bubbly to his Left displayed.

He seems so alike Little Jack Horner:
Stuck in that stark and draughty corner.....
All other tables intended for two:
Pairings old; romances new?

I don't think anyone ever thought
A Single Dinner would by One be sought!
<<Poor fellow! Should we invite him over?>>
<< Not now! He's maybe expecting a Lover?>>

<< But he looks so dreadfully down and lonely!
To-night designed for couples only....?>>
<< We can at least offer him our roses...
And take his photo - if, stood, he poses? >>

Each Feb. I wonder: did Valentine despair
When he looked across to an empty chair?
And how many lasses did he employ:
So parent, unburdened, could share his joy?

ΩΩΩΩΩΩΩΩΩΩΩΩΩΩΩΩ

Introduction to Poem Number Sixteen:

Chistmas decorations make no sense. Some are put up far too early ; removed far too early as well.

Other celebrants of the Twelve Days of Christmas do not take down their trees or their twinkly lights until the thirteenth –occasionally the forty-first! – *day after December* 24th*., the official start of festivities.*

****

SIXTEEN) **TRIMMING UP**

My friend :
Is it too soon, this Noon,
To trim : so grim the weather ?
Never!
Rather, my father used to leave this task -
Such a complicated a task-
To the Eve of the twenty-fifth itself:
The same date many town Shops
Take all evidence of Christmas down!
In an inkling, those twinkling lights extinguished...

The toil of fixing tinsel, paper chains, tin-foil stars;
Gold string the thing to hang up splayed or
Delayed Greeting Cards;
Mixing plaster angels with fragile baubles made of glass, alas;
Chocolate Santas, edible bells, wooden Nativity figures....
I, less agile, wobbling on top rung of shaking ladder,
For my sins: one hand full of hateful drawing-pins....

Goons with festoons, first week in November:
When I'm not ready, second week of December!
Yet how I remember the third day I lit that fat candle:
So quickly aflame, I partly to blame for resulting fire?
Now beginning to tire : soft option, to seize from the Loft
The most real of plastic trees: 'neath which to kneel
To hide five ivy mugs with holly handles:
Each wrapped in crepe and taped: my neat and fleet
Escape from hanging further garlands....

Introduction to Poem Number Seventeen:

Very rarely is my Verse angry. A frequently re-visited exception to my mood mainly undisturbed, unruffled- my dignity, benignity - is the twin phenomenon of Rough Sleeping and Homelessness in all its guises. Conditions usually, perhaps inescapably, accompanied by acute Poverty and despair....

****

SEVENTEEN) **WISE MEN SEEKING WISDOM**

And by the light of one bright star:
Three Wise Men came from country far;
To seek the King was their intent,
And to follow his process wherever it went.

They began by recalling that bare Stable:
Poor housing defeating good tenants able;
Slums, tents, and shacks.... static caravans:
Sofa-surfing, park benches, sleeping at Nan's?

They then considered Income Support:
Households in debt, reserves set at naught.
Parents despairing their children to feed;
Cards, gifts, and treats: what's not to need?

And last they dwelt on raging inflation:
High rates, gas, electric, abandoned vacations?

Not helped by strikes - these many unresolved -
Each year ending in turmoil its challenge revolved.

Nowell, Nowell, Nowell, Nowell,
Hope not extinguished:
A hard message to sell?

Introduction to Poem Number Eighteen:

How fortunate I've been to spend over half my lifetime within half-a-mile of one Primary School or another. And -should the wind carry it across the meadow – the joy of playtime.

****

EIGHTEEN) **SQEALS of DELIGHT ?**

Have you listened?
Have you heard?
The Playground noise
Of Girls & Boys?
These sounds amazingly similar:
From Aldbrough to Scarborough;
From Ottringham to Sandringham;
From Withernsea to Whittlesey.
Those twenty minutes before the Whistle;
Those fifteen minutes of morning Playtime;
Those thirty minutes after Dinner;
Another fifteen minutes during the afternoon:

Squeals of delight: each bouncing-ball in sight;
Energies expended - time-limits slight?
Lots of cheers - mixed twixt occasional tears;
Some children rich ; more children poor
And full of fears
Yet all are welcome through the steel-mesh door.

Oft I ponder when venturing yonder
Why infants at play : some juniors too,
Sound the same
Where'er they're bound?
You'd think they'd make a different noise:
Northampton girls, Southampton boys?

Skipping rope in one yard?
Slipping on puddles hard in another?
Sister in skirt out of tune with brother hurt?
And yet wherever the Playground:
Pupils chanting, panting, telling, yelling, teasing, pleasing,
Really *is* as imitable as: without doubt,
However near, however distant:
Within fencing secure, glee inimitable.

Inroduction to Poem Number Nineteen:

Sometimes the answer to a previously intractable social problem is amazingly simple. You see a deficiency in children's health and welfare; their low morale; their damaged performance; and discover something unexpected - something normally out-of-sight - missing.

It is a platitude that children are our future. Therefore an outlay of just £150 per family here, helping secure that future, comes across as a bargain.

****

NINETEEN) **NO CRIB FOR A BED**

And so to bed:
"A Bed for every Head?"

Instead:
Every Christmas:
Thousands of bairns
Lie down on damp sofa,
Unyielding stone floor?
Scores more
Curled up in a drawer.
While
Older girls doss down in the cellar:
Wisely escaping Mum's new Fella.
Lads in West Park stare up at the stars:
Yet more reclined in junked motor cars;
Other kids restless in sodden tents:
Due to harsh - *and spiralling* - rents?

Anxious children toss and turn
Whilst their Dads more wages earn.
Crumpled children jolt each other:
Soon entombed with weary Mother?

How they grip each threadbare sheet
Longing for some food to eat?
How they clutch coarse blanket stained:
Replacement lost with nothing gained.
And what about those pillows missing:
Whispers soft displaced by hissing?
Truly - incontrovertibly -
Naught for their Comfort.

And what about the next day's dawning:
Brothers wrangling, sisters yawning?
And what about absented schoolrooms;
Lessons lost, detention looming?
Where the exam so early spoiled?
Where the test's in instant foiled?
See the tired cyclist wobbling;
Hear two siblings homeward squabbling.
Find piles of washing unattended,
Repossessions, credit ended.
Each night's sleep unslept;
Each night's dreams undreamt.

Head for bed:
" A Bed for every Head?"

ΩΩΩΩΩΩΩΩΩΩΩΩΩΩΩΩΩΩ

Introduction to Poem Number Twenty

Most Seaside Resorts are not just , by definition, at the end of the line, the terminus for buses. They risk, too, becoming the end of their residents' hopes. Seaside's permanent residents look out to Sea – an undervalued privilege – but must then face coastal visitors staying at home till Easter, then remaining back home from mid-September.

Thus even our greatest Seaside Resorts: the Brightons, Eastbournes and Bournemouths of this Island, contain pockets of deprivation – whilst areas of Blackpool, Great Yarmouth or Rhyll might suffer poverty much deeper and longer: their hotels boarded up, their terraces in disrepair, their sixth-forms disbanded.

In this context, middling Watering Places like Withernsea, Hornsea, Cleethorpes and Bridlington go through stages of both growth and recession adding to their crises of self-confidence; yet still retaining an air of optimism.

****

TWENTY) **SINGING WITHERNSEA's PRAISES**

How shall I sing this Seaside's strengths:
Its sun, its sands, its Prom?
Now is the time to praise at length
Depression emergence from...
So fine these youngsters' theatre, dance,
So unconfined our paeans...

Giving this Town more than mere glance
Broadcasters alerted, keen....

How shall we speak of art & verse:
Guitars beyond compare?
Haddock and Chips,
Each Practice Nurse?
We all our burdens share....
Fresh traders show their offerings,
New shops their wares do ply;
In awe of their profferings ;
Tuppenny Arcades to try!

Hull Road does boast a Lighthouse tall,
A Church and Chapel proud...
Do stop to hear Kay Kendall's call,
More hist'ry spoken loud!
Each terrace is distinctly built:
Bay windows, yellow brick;
And lest enthusiasms wilt,
Tide's turning does the trick .

Introduction to Poem Number Twenty-One

Any Verse written for – or even at the same time as – Remembrance Sunday must address Warfare and its horrific repercussions not only for soldiers stationed overseas but also for the bombed-out or malevolently occupied Homeland.

The challenge then is to address death – widespread mortality - with sensitivity. And the key to unlocking this particular effort is remembering how words taken from Psalm 113 can have two completely separate interpretations.

****

TWENTY-ONE) **At the GOING DOWN of the SAME**

Mons, Marne, Cambrai, Caporetto:
Remember.
Amiens, Argonne, Isonzo, Gallipoli:
Remember.
Verdun, Vimy Ridge, Jutland, Somme:
Remember.
Ludendorff, Tannenberg and Ypres:
Remember.
Remember those who fell
At the going down of the same.

Anzio, Atlantic, Bulge and Berlin:
Remember.
Kursk, Kharkov, Crete and Dunkirk:
Remember.
Midway and Moscow, Monte Casino:
Remember.
Leningrad, Normandy, Pearl Harbour:
Remember.
Stalingrad, Okinawa and No Man's Land:
Remember.

Remember those who fell
At the going down of the same.

Fell suddenly?
Fell hastily?
Fell needlessly?
Fell Irretrievably?
And irrecoverably.
Fell gloriously?
Fell ignominiously?
Falling unnamed?
Falling unmourned?

Yet still we are bidden to remember;
Remember those who fell
At the going down of the same.

ΩΩΩΩΩΩΩΩΩΩΩΩΩΩΩΩΩΩ

Introduction to Poem Number Twenty-Two

Everybody knows somebody who purchases –or has delivered– daily Newspapers, local or national, regional or international, free or paid for. But are these Papers always opened? In which case....?

****

TWENTY-TWO) **FEAR of MISSING OUT ?**

Seated at the occasional table
Where occasionally she sat
I noted a pile of Weekend newspapers
Saturday or Sunday newspapers
Neatly folded - yet, critically, unread
Unread yet still neatly folded
Even the Critics unread
Critics of Radio, TV, Cinema, the Arts
Unread
Critics of Opera, Pop, Books and Sport
Each unread...

So was the buyer of these weighty Supplements
Unread
In her bedstead, dead?
Or was she waiting, one day,
To read them, leisurely, instead?
Or did she of no cross words
Buy them simply for their Crosswords?
Puzzles perhaps not so simple ?
Or were these Papers' more for Programmes?
Programmes coming to the BBC?
Programming forthcoming no longer?
Each paper's purchase then intended
To keep one Trader trading
At profit
His critical profit
A profit
At least on paper?

Introduction to Poem Number Twenty-Three

Anybody starting their own business – especially when that business is also their house – as Office, Warehouse or Guest House – risks failure, round-the-clock working hours, even repossession, because they have used that home as collateral security for their start-up loan. In other words, the risk is ever present & unevenly spread. The sharp end of this "modern-day slavery" I observed in the once-flourishing Boarding House I happened to stay in thrice in order to visit relatives in the Home Counties.

Hence this analysis, literally at close quarters.

****

TWENTY-THREE) **DOWN IN A MINUTE**

"It's still quite early for bacon-and-eggs
Preceding rush hour for our legs!
Soon seeking porridge, Emmanuel Hall...
At Table Twelve: Lavinia Mc.Call...
And Father Fox will be down in a mo?
Pity our lass Carmen is a no-show !
While all is peace on the upper floor
Where I leave brown toast outside the door."

" Is that the telephone ringing urgent
Just when the dishes need detergent?
New bookings often fall to me

Seeing what bedrooms might be free."
" This late July is everso busy...
But hold on a sec: I'll speak to Lizzy..
We could have had a cancellation:
Someone with a sick relation?
Yes I've got a very nice Suite...
Where newlyweds enamoured meet..."

Me and Lizzy were doing fine:
Local cuisine, finest wine.
Then Weekly Lets made great inroads
Our balance sheet, once black, implodes.
<<Air bnb>>: it stole our trade
Trashing the upgrades we have made.
Folk choose the freedom of self-cater:
Redundancy for Charles our Waiter.
They even pay our Cleaner more:
Operating <<Within the Law>>.

Introduction to Poem Number Twenty-Four

When I arrived at King's Cross Railway Station, from Hull, one Winter morning, I was amazed just how many of the Capital's Policemen, and Police vehicles, were filling the road crossing to St. Pancras International, bang opposite, had assembled simply on the off-chance of an avowedly peaceful Protest March passing.

Overkill?

In any case, the scene that day set me thinking about all *Processions: Processions that in several parts of the world – Burma? China? Iran? Mexico? – would not only be deemed illegal - but would also result in the immediate shooting down of innocent Processors.*

****

TWENTY-FOUR) **PROCESSIONS STILL PROCEEDING ?**

The King has spoken,
The Nation awoken?
On the day of Coronation:
Not One Procession but Two
To greet our Monarch new....
To the Abbey one cheering crowd;
Back to the Palace, more shouting loud.

But what of other Processions :
Long marches ; fewer possessions?
Hundreds of people following:
No lies, nor bunkum, swallowing?

With' itself held a mighty outpouring:
All previous gath'rings outscoring;
The whole Town reduced to mourning:
One coffin life-save flags adorning.
To Left & Right much doleful weeping;

Out at Sea careful watches keeping.

Wooden oars held bolt upright:
Pier Towers kept ever in sight.
Friends and family dressed respectfully;
Cameras not purring neglectfully.

The next big Procession will be in France?
Lest retirement age they advance?
Protests round Incineration...?
Always risking Incarceration?

Introduction to Poem Number Twenty-Five

Ever since my first conscious turning of the page at Midnight on December 31st. leading into a brand new year, I have been influenced – captivated – by Hymns or Verse written specifically for this Milestone.

Therefore, when I knew The Holderness Gazette was going to publish very early the following Year, I turned my attention to all the possibilities....

****

TWENTY-FIVE) **ANOTHER YEAR IS DAWNING**

Another Year is dawning:
Endowed with hope and light?
Another Year where warnings
Of Doom are put to flight?

Another Year of Progress
From where we stood before;
Another Year of Congress,
Friendship - and Peace, not War.

Another Year of Prizes
Obtained by one and all?
A Year when chance arises
To hear the clarion call.

Another Year of striving:
For some, against the odds?
A Year when gains arriving
Pour down from stranger gods.

Another Year agreeing
On goals beyond our helm?
Another Year of seeing
What debts might overwhelm.

Another Year is dawning:
High Tides approaching Shore?
A Year our lives adorning:
New language - and new lore.

Acknowledging Frances Ridley Havergal

Introduction to Poem Number Twenty-Six

When you're walking, you exist with a constant state of alertness. This awareness is not necessarily conscious: more the memory of all walks that have gone before this walk; any viewpoints or For Sale Notices; any diversions or habits. And a large proportion of daily walks, even on holiday, follow - or help to - construct habit.

On my unhurried *walks, I pay particular attention to discarded trifles, attempting to ask that question born of curiosity: just* why *did* that *get left behind?*

****

TWENTY-SIX) **A TALE of TWO DUMMIES**

Now lost to their Mummies:
Two plastic Dummies.

Not lost on the Prom -
[Where Mummies do meet]
But cast to one side
[Where nine toddlers reside]
On parallel Street:
Let's meet our Guide!

Two anxious Mummies
Bought two soothing Dummies

To keep offspring quiet -
Not causing a riot!

But both bairns rejected
What soon they ejected
From the two baby-carriages
Giv'n for two recent marriages!

Or?

One babe enraged -
And in Bedlam engaged -
Pink Dummy discarded
As this he regarded
Both gross interference
And cissy appearance.

His Gran bought a second
[She harassed, still fecund?]
This time in *blue*:
[A more comforting hue? -
But equally nasty
To boy craving pasty!]

Now trace these two Dummies
Unclean;
By three anxious Mummies unseen!

Introduction to Poem Number Twenty-Seven:

Light shines in darkness: principally the Sun and the Moon. But competing with Nature's magic is the presence – often the nuisance - of light pollution. Admittedly some of this artificial light is beneficial: for public safety or the reduction of crime; or the floodlighting of football pitches, warehouse yards and airstrips.

****

TWENTY-SEVEN) **LET THERE BE LIGHT!**

From Valley Gardens' tree
Light shines.
From a thousand smaller trees
Light shines.
From the Queen's Nursing Home
Light shines.
From the top of the Lighthouse
Light shines.
From Aldi's late-night shop
Light shines.
From the municipal Swimming-pool
Light shines.
From homework marked in High School
Light shines.
From many an awoken bedroom
Light shines.

From the fascia of our Meridian Centre
Light shines.
From many a kindly face
Light shines.
Light shines in darkness
And the darkness comprehends it not.

Introduction to Poem Number Twenty-Eight

Here an overtly humorous Poem: written after hearing a Train Announcement out of Hull, early one Saturday Morning.

****

TWENTY-EIGHT) **WELCOME ON BOARD....**

"Hello! I'm Mrs. Quest: your Train Manager.
And this is the 09-09 *TransPennine* train
From Hull to Liverpool.
Please check that your Ticket states *Liverpool*
Not Hartlepool or Pontypool,
Blackpool or Welshpool.

"We welcome on board, too,
Mrs.Root our Driver,
Mrs.Sharpe our Ticket-Collector,
Mrs. Drinkwater our Catering Manager -
And Mrs. Garner our Litter-Collector.

" Relax now and look out for the Humber Bridge
And the Ouse Bridge;
Gilberdyke & Aberfordyke;
Mirfield & Huddersfield.
Meanwhile I omitted to welcome Mrs.Plant
On Board: our Plate-layer and Lookout."

Introduction to Poem Number Twenty-Nine :

Some years are definitely wetter than others; equally, some Seasons are wetter – or drier – than others. But what happens when the Heavens open and will not close? Not only are holidays, shopping trips and commutes spoiled by downpours; sports fixtures are postponed – and whole livelihoods are threatened.

****

TWENTY-NINE) **LONG TO RAIN OVER US**

Christmas crispy with white frost:
Instead - and at what a cost?-
It rains.
It rains and rains and rains and rains.
Christmas carpets of deep snow:
Instead - and see wild rivers flow! -
It rains.
It rains and rains and rains and rains.
Christmas slips on shining ice:
Instead - not twice, but thrice -
It rains,
It rains and rains and rains and rains.

As the Heavens open wide
Little children rise to abide
Cold and freezing rain:
Rain no Parka can keep out;
Rain to make street traders doubt
Cash-flow's show of loss or gain?
Rain though many doorways creeping;
Rain through many windows seeping;
Rain to halt the sun a-peeping;
Rain so many gutters deep'ning;
Rain delaying bus and train;
Rain each cyclist to detrain.

Will this rainfall ever stop?
All defences overtop?
Will wet ground take any more?
Parsnips ruined before store?
Will green sprouts be gathered in?
Sale of caulies rather thin?
Will red spuds fill many pails?
Daffodils withstand the gales?
Where the swedes of weight and size?
Where the leeks to win top prize?
In the rain are all things blighted;
In harsh deluge, all benighted.

Introduction to Poem Number Thirty

Sending Christmas Cards is fun as well as – for some people - an annual chore. *Some correspondents send cardboard cards* and *e-cards; some choosing one format above the other. Whilst a third group of people send none at all - despite being glad to receive them.*

Here, as I take down my Christmas decorations, I turn my mind to folk I perhaps should have gone out of my way to include on my lengthening Card List?

****

THIRTY) **LEST I FORGOT**
(Regrets, 11pm., January 6th.)

Will the list ever end
Of Christmas Cards
I *failed* to send?

The Mother of my Cleaner
(Could anything be meaner?)
The Sister of my Plumber
(Leaving her much glummer?)
The Butcher's aproned Daughter
(So many hens to slaughter?)
The Lifeguard's ailing Aunt
(Afford the stamp you can't?)
My Neighbour's helpful Son
(Awkward battles won?)
The Uncle of our Priest
(His work-load so increased?)
The Bus Driver's ailing Granny
(Also his loyal Nanny?)
Our Newsagent's delivery lad
(*And* his anxious Grand-dad?)

The Baker's hotplate girl
(Of great price, sure, the Pearl?)
The Landlord's weary Staff)
(Those making us Punters laugh?)
Young Mildred's Science Teachers
(Dissecting all God's Creatures?)

All these did I forget:
Their festive cheer unmet?

Introduction to Poem Number Thirty-One

Here I return to a familiar theme: detritus dropped before I pass it by. What on Earth (literally?) could be its significance or its value?

****

THIRTY-ONE) **THE MISSING PIECE....**

In the very corner of a very sodden Bus Shelter:
Two bedraggled, peeling, pieces of a Jigsaw Puzzle.
Were these two pieces willfully removed
Before the sealing of that Puzzle
For Greyhound Rescue?

Or did the absence of those 2 particular pieces
Ruin one child's happiness completing –

Competing ?
Or almost completing the whole?

And then I trod more the puddled highway South
And met - or rather *didn't meet* -
A second muddled - or befuddled? - benefactor:
He - or was it she? -
Who scattered random Playing Cards
Along the kerbs, and into the gutters:
Utterly alone, not in tandem...

Did this person, at best
Suffer from an incomplete *fifty-two*?
And therefore need rid of the rest?
Or was this the setting for some sort of test?
Local Dads, local kids, picking up
First a Jack, and then a Queen, and then a King?
Unless the Joker should turn out to have been
The unseen one who chose to scatter
In the first place?

I do not know if I shall play
Whist or Bridge, Palace, Piquet, Pitch or Blitz -,
The dummy Card in Rummy? -
The elusive Ace of Spades? -
With Playing Cards rescued from degeneration?
Or shall I need a brand new pack:
One purchased from Greyhound Rescue?

Introduction to Poem Number Thirty-Two

Ever since the 1980s there have been questions around the thousands – even millions – of people not able to join in technological advance. Through old age? Through Poverty? Through complexity? Maybe through a bad experience with it? Scams. Fraud. More likely distrust that Big Tech will do all it promises to do?

And wider society – younger society? – appears to take pity on their parents, fellow citizens, neighbours or colleagues suffering from techno-fear or digital exclusion. In this Poem I try to imagine how it is possible simply to slip into the great unknown: maybe owning not a smart-phone. Perdition?

****

THIRTY-TWO) **DIGITALLY EXCLUDED ?**

Let me tell you the tale of Simone:
One young lady with no Phone.
She reaching the age of Twenty:
Surely with options plenty?
But her mother once active and fair
Now languishes in wheelchair;
Leaving this only Daughter
To complete all the chores that were taught her:
The washing and ironing and cleaning;
Bathing Mum - plus toilet - demeaning?
Finance and shopping and mending;
To Gran's needs, also, attending.

She smallest Care Grant claiming:
Neighbours her "idleness" blaming!

Simone cut off from any e-mail
Leads any job-search to fail.
And prevented from going to College
Leaves her short of quantum new knowledge.
While distance from each social medium
Leaves her stranded in seven-day tedium.
She unable to win any Boy-friend
Till Mother's spoon-feed should end.
At least Mother's Mother can't ring her:
So someone a penned note must bring her.
Now even the telly is broken
Not helping this Sludgebump awoken.

Without a smart-phone to hand
She's building her fortress on sand.
And short of glitz websites to visit
"*Silence is golden*" - or is it?
Our world belongs to the Surfers:
Dubbed the locked-out: "*Flat Earthers*."
Could Simone not get *a land-line*?
Why BT's pound-a-day decline?
And *if* she buys Broadband as well :
Providers their profits can swell!
Simpler a small laptop to get?
But how will *connecting* be met?

Best leave Simone on the margin:
Her struggles with Debt not enlarging?

Introduction to Poem Number Thirty-Three

I've always had some sort of relationship with Scooters: starting with scooting along a quiet roadway at the back of our terraced house in Longton. That Scooter obtained second-hand through a postcard pinned to our newsagent's window: and powered by my bent right leg.

Much later in life, my viewpoint on Scooters solidified as more and more of these Machines became available: some posing great danger *to Pedestrians like me; others more benign – nonetheless, very fast!*

****

THIRTY-THREE) **THE SEVEN AGES OF SCOOTER**

The *First* Age of Scooter is also a stage:
A lively toddler's toy
With three wheels not two:
Of polythene, new.

The *Second* Age of Scooter
Is both thrifty and nifty:
Familiar in Nineteen-Fifty -
And before! Propelled solely
By handlebar, and Right leg wholly:
Till a *Third* Age dawned: tracing
The Electric Scooter racing
On "Private Land" - except
By Government Scheme embracing
Appointed pick-ups and drop-offs:
Here your Right Leg idle for longer.

For it is the *stronger* School Leaver
From Venice, Valletta?
Mounting the *Fourth* Scooter:
A *Vespa, Lambretta*?
Much better for obligations given:
Wider platform, petrol driven.
But Riders: be Ye not cowered
By bigger Motorbikes, higher powered?
Yamaha?, Honda?
From Italy, India, yonder….

Which leads us to the the *Fifth* Age of Scooter:
The fairway buggy
For the fifteenth hole its golf clubs hugging.
Taking us soon to the *Sixth* Age of Scooter,
The Mobility Tricycle,
At six miles an hour
Faster than a bicycle - and steady:
Ready for the *Seventh* Age of Scooter:
Solid, chunky, adored;
Twin-doored?
No way , this time, to be ignored;
Four-wheeled - and for the well-heeled:
Rather like the Motorcar, a Star!
Charged to go far.

ΩΩΩΩΩΩΩΩΩΩΩΩΩΩΩΩΩ

Introduction to Poem Number Thirty-Four

If there was a separate classification: "nostalgic and sentimental" : this Verse would definitely be filed thereunder.

Because here I try to remember just how I got down to the Beach – rushed down to the Beach – as a young boy, full of excitement. And those Seaside Resort staircases stuck in my memory long enough for all *future outdoor staircases – poolside, lakeside, urban, countryside: each run holding almost something like that same fascination, including counting the number of steps, and tackling the best barefoot.*

Most elusive are the Belvederes, particularly the Belvederes in the grounds of Stately Homes: solid stone Platforms accessed by exactly the same number of pulpit steps to the Left and to the Right.

****

THIRTY-FOUR)

I MUST GO DOWN TO THE SEA AGAIN

Where the Bay?
Where the Beach?
Where the Sands I dare to reach?
Where delightful gap in Wall discovered?
Where the Steps with moss & slime o'ercovered?

Twist and turn,
Turn then twist:
So much to learn?
Rough concrete cleverly disguised,
By all but fishermen despised?
Coarse gravel showing through -
In case the knave he tempted be ?
Brief Platform:
Then Stairs down twenty -
Plenty: these built from Right to Left.
Brief Platform two,
Down twenty narrow footholds more:
These now from Left to Right-
To Sea-Wall clinging tight-
Like blackened arrow pointing at the Waves -
Davy Jones's euphemistic grave? -
Fourteen or more for half of each day hidden:
Me bidden, they forbidden?

Yet there are other gaps-
Clearer, wider, fierce Ocean in their sight:
Ramps for little boats of pleasure,
Picnics, swimming, reading, leisure.
Added to by newer Steps:
These, fewer, climbing upward first
To broader Platform;
Then twenty down between the rocks -
Ideal for absent shoes and socks -
To broader Platform two.
From there a final score or more -
Observed far more from safer Shore? -
To reach a sandier beach.

Introduction to Poem Number Thirty-Five

When I was young, Withernsea had no dedicated Lifeboat – but that deficit was remedied in 1974 when a brand new Station was built on South Cliff.

Coincidentally, celebrations of 50 years returning here, Year 2024 came at the same time R.N.L.I. nationally was marking its 200th. Anniversary of outreach. This Anniversary I decided to approach more numerically than sentimentally.

****

THIRTY-FIVE) **CELEBRATING the R.N.L.I.'s 200th.**

Congratulations, Coxswains: two hundred years old this week.
Congratulations, too, 4 times 200 Women Lifeboat Crew.
Your 238 Lifeboat Stations: look to windswept *Withernsea*
Whose own Lifeboat Station is 50 years old this year.
And your 2 times 200 Lifeboats take pride
At 2 times 200 lives saved last year, waves defied.

Then mourn your 60 Lifeboats lost
During those 200 Years of shipping tossed.
To find that 600 Lifeboat men, Sea conditions poor,
Never made it back in time to Shore:
Sure, too, that for 60 years now
60 Lifeboats - *and more?* - became swifter, lighter.

And your 50 times 200 loyal, *royal*, Volunteers rejoice:
The Lord be praised!
All the money you've raised
To keep this show on the silver surf:
And your Seaside guards: as training teaches-
Now patrol 200 - *and 50 more* - holiday Beaches.
Your organization, ever unfailing,
Aids those - *too soon* – into peril sailing.

Introduction to Poem Number Thirty-Six

In some very posh neighbourhoods of London, Georgian or Edwardian front entrances are remarkably high and distinguished: sometimes reached by two or three steps.

So on my morning walks, I was surprised to discover ten or eleven similarly lofty front doors on one street in Withernsea. Were these grand entrances a relic of the Resort's unfulfilled attempt to imitate Brighton, Southwold or Aberaeron? Or the legacy of the enterprising master builders who built 90% of Withernsea's original terraces? At cost.

****

THIRTY- SIX) **A VERY TALL ORDER**

Tallboys, tall hats, tall ships, tall stories;
Walk tall...but how tall?
And what about tall doorways:
Entrances far higher, taller than any conventional doorway?

These not six-foot-six; more eight-foot-eight.
And it's to Withernsea's *Queen Street North*
We must head for that extra headroom.

It is the Chancellor who talks of
The headroom he or she needs to cut taxation.
And on the top decks of East Yorkshire buses
Tall boys, tall men, are told of their limited headroom.
And at the entry to each Municipal Car Park,
The famed <Max Headroom>
Turns back advancing caravans all.

Back on Withernsea's *Queen Street North*:
What foresight? What imagination?
What artistry? What over-arching ambition:
Crafting doorways so mighty; so distinguished;
So utterly *unexpected?* So *expensive*?
So expansive a concept - except in a Bath or Belgravia;
Unseen, except in majestic Resorts, South Coast.

And how is it such a modest retreat as this -
A Settlement so literally at the End-of-the-Line -
Should attract such remarkable - and capable - Builders?
Not just those Builders by Anthony Bannister summoned;
Not cheapskate Builders - Speculators without scruple -
But Jobbing Builders, Master Builders, with enterprise:
Joiners joining in to install entrances *so invitingly tall.*

ΩΩΩΩΩΩΩΩΩΩΩΩΩΩΩΩΩΩ

Introduction to Poem Number Thirty-Seven

This Story was amazingly easy to commit to paper – because it was founded, and inspired, by my real-life experience: a comical, definitely not a tragic, experience.

Much of daily life is humorous. The only difficulty relating an anecdote such as the recollection that follows as prose, rather than Verse, is the possibility of it falling flat. That is why too many writers or public speakers whose content is solely anecdotal suffer overkill.

****

THIRTY-SEVEN) **FOOTLOOSE and FREE ?**

Imagine arriving in Ottringham or Keyingham?
In Bilton or in Preston?
In Anlaby or Willerby?
By Train in Crewe - or Timbuktu?
With one Shoe
But also *without one Shoe* ?

My functioning shoe proves most efficient -
But on this day: not quite sufficient?
Its mate of sole now deficient:
Over every pebble creaking,
Sunk in every puddle, leaking.

In wayside shoe-shop now I'm seated:
By eighteen boxes undefeated;
My purse by thirty pounds depleted?
Actually wearing my *new* shoe,
Replacing that for dust-cart due!

But still the Till Girl's unbelieving:
My wearing new shoe, she deceiving?
She thirty pounds short receiving?
Thus she seeks in sand a footprint -
Lest re-shod down street I sprint?

Upright reader: please show some care
For he who now wears mismatched pair!

Introduction to Poem Number Thirty-Eight

This Poem is a mixture of disappointment and startlement: my fervent wish for a creeping social custom to die – which is peculiar in the light of Death its Subject?

There is a very real danger Poetry might be used first for campaigning, second for preaching. But two Poets far more skilled than me: Thomas Hardy and Thomas Hood have definitely strayed into this territory without sacrificing artistry.

****

THIRTY-EIGHT) **THE WAKE THAT NEVER SLEEPS**

In the morning, mourning?
A passing too soon?
Remembered at Noon.
No chance his life forgetting
At the Sun's setting?
Reverence done right:
All through the Night?

In the South, Portsmouth:
But surely not in Hornsea -
Or in Withernsea?
At Runnymede solemnly decreed:
But surely not in Hornsea –
Or in Withernsea?
On the Great Orme - alert to artillery's storm:
But surely not in Hornsea –
Or in Withernsea?
So many names: repeat them
At the National Arboretum
Throughout the bombed Metropolis
Aloft in Scotch Necropolis
But surely not in Hornsea
Or in Withernsea?

Yet to one wooden Bench
Turned, wistfully, out toward Sea:

Bring the Wembley scarf
So proudly worn by him
Throughout each second-half.
Bring lilies and pot-plants;
His childhood toys;
His underpants?
Bring photos and hit single
Worth singing on the shingle?
Bring Cards and Birthday Greetings
Recalling erstwhile Meetings?
In fact bring *everything*:
Woven wreath or scented rose,
Lachrymose.

And make this morticed Bench
A memory of the wrench
His family felt
At such a sudden parting:
One curious habit starting.

Introduction to Poem Number Thirty-Nine

There was a time not so long ago when Teachers in certain Local Authorities had to declare any Gifts – or hand them back!

Fortunately perhaps, modern regulations are far more generous, therefore far more logical. Provided Teachers only accept trifles (not literally!); and provided they never treat their Pupils better or worse in response to pay-offs given or withheld, they can accept those end-of-term, or end-of-year, Gifts with a clear conscience.

****

THIRTY-NINE) **EGGING EACH OTHER ON?**

Twenty out of his Thirty-One
Realize Easter had just begun
And buy their Teacher -
Just for fun?
Or to pull his leg?
Each, a sparkling Easter Egg.

Alf buys Cadbury; Sarah buying Fry;
Anne her egg: filled with *Galaxy*.
John buys *Snickers*, Jane something thicker:
A whole Terry's Orange, and *not* some *Milky Bar* white.
[Lindt a bit classier in their Teacher's sight?]

Very soon, Mr. Addams is bursting at the seams:
Turning his back on *Smarties*, even *M&Ms*!
Which Charity might take *Buttons*?
And which *Celebrations*?
Soon to go *Aero*;
Next Gold *Ferrero...*
[The Easter break, chance for deliberation?]

But then Victor arrives at Mr. Addams' door
With a prize that shakes his Teacher to the core:
An Easter Garden on a plywood base,
Pilate denying Christ a last-minute pardon...
[Next term's lesson will look into the case?]

Beyond: three wooden crosses;
Two villains have time to count their losses;
Eleven wee disciples drawing nigh
To see their Master strung up high.
[Victor now victorious?
His classmates running shy?]

<u>Introduction to Poem Number Forty</u>

This Poem was composed before the invasion of incomprehensible - and far more difficult to reproduce - QR Codes.

But the barcodes QR seeks to replace are themselves relatively new: Year 1972 onward. And how successful those barcodes were – and are! Barcodes are so individual, they go through a shop till rapidly enough to inform the shopkeeper exactly what he has sold; and his wholesaler or Head Office which items to despatch.

In this Poem I try to retrieve a whole life of "three-score-years-and-ten defined by barcode."

****

FORTY) **PASSING THROUGH LIFE BY BARCODE**

Each newborn babe in her Cradle
Round her wrist carries a Label:
The NHS's Barcode

Each Scholar after Soccer
Opens his personal Locker:
By keying in a Barcode

Each Student plating Dinner:
Chicken Pie the clearest Winner?
Her Lanyard: a Barcode

Each Young Offender's rankle
Is the Tag around his Ankle:
Monitored by a Barcode

Each Newlywed's Bedroom entry:
In the absence of a Sentry
Comes through her key fob's Barcode

Each Shopper's visit to Store:
Her bulging Trolley - and more -
Is paid for scanning Barcodes

Each Worker's Clocking out -
Shift's ending coming about -
Swiping a Barcode

Each Pensioner's foreign flight -
His suitcase now out of sight -
Redirected via Barcode

Each Patient's laying to rest:
In Mortuary, lightly dressed?
Goes identified with a Barcode!

ΩΩΩΩΩΩΩΩΩΩΩΩΩΩΩΩΩ

Introduction to Poem Number Forty-One

Few shipping routes are as well known as the North of England's sea link with Rotterdam, thence to Amsterdam. This operated by P&O's overnight Ferries to and from Hull Docks: a service operated alternately by two mighty ships: "Pride of Rotterdam" and "Pride of Hull."

And one day, or rather one evening, I found myself a one-way foot passenger on the "Pride of Hull."

****

FORTY-ONE) **<< THE PRIDE OF HULL >>**

The Ship's already in the Port,
Long lorries beginning to board;
Maersk Containers on deck to sort -
And then mounts the Golden Horde.

This is a Leisure Sector huge:
With thousands of pounds to spend;
Full Coaches dumping one human deluge;
Car drivers, lane markings attend.

A hi-vis Crew identity proves:
Each paid not the minimum wage;
Anxious Infants summoned to soothe,
Ascending the thirteenth stage.

The lifting of heavy anchors due:
Five guide-ropes wound promptly in;
Rusting gang-planks raised anew;
Ten turbines creating a din.

On Sale Heaven Scent, Vodka and Whisky,
Costa coffee in frothing mugs;
Jangling bandits tempting the risky;
Teenagers waiting for hugs.

After much Song and stuttering Dance
A Gong does our Bed-time announce;
"Give tired heads a slumbering chance
And don't let your Canines pounce."

At Nine in the morning, tapping and shouts:
" We must clean your Cabin now!"
" Claim your stalled Waggon, one way out-
And future Patronage vow."

Introduction to Poem Number Forty-Two

Hull City Centre – about 18 miles West of Withernsea – is nothing if it isn't the Capital of closed Department Stores, replaced in savvy shoppers' patronage with smaller and fitter bargain basements: some of these themselves shut. Here is the Story, indeed the legacy, of one particular famous name now no more.

****

FORTY-TWO)

On SHUTTING our DOORS for the LAST TIME

"Please ring for Attention;"
Minimal your detention?
Did no one our closure mention?
Our Signage deserving retention?
"Please ring for Attention."

You're standing in our Car Park;
Redundant our lowliest Clerk;
Our Managers' prospects stark;
Each Night-time very dark:
In our lonely store Car Park.

Big shoes, and large plot, to fill?
If Town Planners have the will?
Pop-up Christmas could fit the bill?
One wing an *Express Grill*?
A difficult plot to fill.

Boots, NEXT, have a lot more glamour;
Posh shops bought under the hammer?
Hull could do with a new Slammer?
AMAZON entering our Grammar;
Retail Parks with a lot more glamour.

Are we silly to want a new Tenant?
Same Staff - but a different Pennant?
John Lewis a "Noughties" Remnant?
Trampolines a bit more relevant?
Attracting an alternative Tenant.

Keep ringing to alert us;
The Internet wants to pervert us;
Our Customers bound to desert us;
A Fire Sale arranged to divert us;
Keep trying to alert us

Maybe halt when you notice our Bell:
Head Office: eighty Sites to sell?
Bare Departments feel like Hell?
Rough Sleepers now we repel?
Pause for thought when you notice our Bell?

__Introduction to Poem Number Forty-Three__

An absolutely intriguing question : where did Motor Caravans, Caravans containing an integral engine, come from? This question is always uppermost in Seaside Resorts, at lakesides, also just outside big tourist traps like Edinburgh, Chester, Oxford or Stratford-upon-Avon, where these mobile hotel rooms need to park.

And like all invasive hobbies, invasive vehicles too, Motor Caravans spawn – encourage? – equal measures of love or hatred.

****

FORTY-THREE) **ASLEEP at the WHEEL?**

It was in the Year 1900
That the first tired traveller
Put pallet and pack in the back
Of his Car - newly invented -
And, much contented,
Fell asleep at the wheel.

And it was in the Year 1910
That Pierce-Arrow's Landau:
A very upright vehicle
Would endow Holidaymakers -
Of Motels forsakers -
Their first Motor Home.

And it was in the Year 1947
That Mr. Pon came upon
The Volkswagen chassis
That allowed lads or lasses
To fall asleep at the wheel
Of their first Dormobile.

And it was in the Year 2023
That Annette bought her first Vanette;
That Aaron drove far in his Homecar;
That Ali conquered damp in her Bush-Camp;
That Alistair showed thrift in his Swift;
That Abbey ate sago in her Winnebego;
That Alan set the timer in his Hymer;
That Amy found Arcadia in her Adria;
That Alf sold debenture to afford his Venture;
That Asher sipped Lambrusco in her Etrusco;
That Adam strung streamer in his Dreamer;
That Ada played Cello in her Morello;
Archie biscuit dunking in his Sun King.

Many the Trippers sea-breezes to feel.
Many those Families asleep at the wheel.

Introduction to Poem Number Forty-Four:

Fog is less common these days: partly as a result of clean-air legislation. But at the Seaside, a different type of fog drifts in from the Sea: impenetrable for the first couple of miles – whilst Villages only a little inland bask in wonderful Sunshine.

****

FORTY-FOUR) **THE HAAR**

It drifts in unexpectedly:
The Haar.
It drifts in heavily:
The Haar.
It drifts in coolly:
The Haar.
It drifts in conclusively:
The Haar.
Dense fog
Drifting Eastwards -
Later North-Eastwards -
From a chill Sea:
Blanketing Withernsea
And Hornsea, and Bridlington;
Blanking out completely
Each carefully-planned plan;
Blanking out completely
The play of playing children;
Blanking out completely
The picnics of picnicking Families;

Blanking out completely
The hopes of hopeful Holidaymakers:
Haar drifting in from afar.

And under its discomforting white blanket:
The Haar that distinguishes May
May extinguish Summer?

Introduction to Poem Number Forty-Five

Anybody who loves "ancient" films remembers those Carriages trundling over cobbles. And there are remarkably few Towns and Villages left without TV aerials or satellite dishes, where modern film Directors can set up Set.

In fact, Carriages are amazingly romantic: embedded as they are in lives lived before Railways; the history of the Royal Mail; and the ambushes of Highwaymen. Principally, occupied by Royalty.

****

FORTY-FIVE) **CARRIAGES AT ELEVEN**

A Challenge never ceasing:
Baggage not decreasing.
Weighting without measure;
Trekking with no pleasure.
Just how to carry a Child
(One neither meek - nor mild?)

Just nine months after marrying
Comes the complex task of carrying
A babe so newly born
(Pink woolly onesie worn);
His Siblings too
(By rain soaked through)
All needing extra shopping;
Past all distractions hopping.

"*Silver Cross*" provides solution:
Posh Pram - with no pollution.
Or Maclaren Buggy folding; -
(Round Toddler's bottom moulding).
One Buggy for the edibles?
Four for Quads, incredible!
And still there's space for Willy
(On Invalid's lap so silly)
As Gran's Scooter gathers speed
(No other kids to heed?)

You could, of course, use shoulders:
(Enchanting all Beholders?)
Or grab a Tesco trolley
(Hand free, unfurling brolly?)
Adopt Cyclist's wicker-basket
(Risking that funeral casket?)
Better still: a Bicycle trailer
(Harnessed sure, preventing failure?)
Some dragged carts carry five!
(While all their Mothers strive

To shut out the differing views of
Wives who Child-freedom choose?)

And don't ignore the Seaside Donkey
Carrying littl'uns a wee-bit wonky;
Or why not make the Rascals walk
As soon as they have learnt to talk?

Introduction to Poem Number Forty-Six

Most people have areas of life they are either missing out on or have missed out on. And some of these areas are never, ever, discovered, less inhabited.

In this autographical Poem, I find Music I have never heard before; or which I have heard before but only in the background; or Music I have heard once or twice before and then spurned. This in modern parlance called "a journey."

****

FORTY-SIX) **THE SOUND OF MUSIC**

All that Jazz?
No trumpeters round here, Mate...
Popular music bypassed my childhood:
Some Brahms, no harm;
And a bit of Elgar with my *Welgar*
(Welwyn Gardens' Shredded Wheat)
Presented neat, followed by a few Hymns.

And in Mid-life
Some Handel longside candles -
Lo *The Seekers* through one speaker;
And the *Sound of Music*:
(Of Lloyd-Webber, no refusenik);
Cliff Richard very daring!
Mantovani the least wearing,
And "*One Hundred Best Tunes*."

But then in Old Age
Country & Western's revelation;
Elation, Dolly Parton: elation!
Leading on to Johnny Cash -
Joan Baez not the least bit rash -
Even some Elvis, coiffured;
(Shakin' Stevens' tracks procured)
Plus the treat of *Spice Girls*, nice.

Train now to Merseyside
For a *Beatles'* Tour:
That most famous Four
I should have embraced -
With *The Hollies* interlaced -
Guitarists my new inspiration
(Roy Orbison hardly displaced)
Neil Diamond's accreditation.
So whatever *next*?

ΩΩΩΩΩΩΩΩΩΩΩΩΩΩΩΩΩΩ

Introduction to Poem Number Forty-Seven

Because Queueing is such an essential ingredient of modern life – car drivers spend on average eighty-four wasted hours per year in traffic jams – Queueing makes an ideal subject for Verse. Not only because, in a long Queue the versifier has plenty of time to devote to composition!

****

FORTY-SEVEN) **QUEUEING, QUEUEING, QUEUEING**

If only there were fewer
In front of me:
Most impatient Queuer!
Its lead now out-of-sight:
Has she been here all last night?
This Queue is not for Sport:
For Wimbledon's Centre Court;
Nor for a Football Match,
One famed Player a goal to snatch?
Nor even for fast Fairground Ride:
Most promised excitement denied?

No: *my* Queues are very chance:
Chance yet my hours to enhance!
My Queues are "unexpected":
By Computer undetected.
In *Tesco* a girl still at Lunch:
Shoppers beginning to bunch;

At the Bus Stop a load of Scholars;
At Passports' some untrained wallah?
At the Post Office presents unweighed:
To Fiji or Faro delayed.

And what of the cussed queuer:
Whose "slight hitch" could not be truer?
Who's carrying the wrong type of money
For his sausage and porridge and honey?
Whose smart-phone signal's too faint;
Whose Toddler's beyond restraint?
Who's lost the key to his chariot:
And turned up at Hilton not Marriott?
Whose problems defy all solution -
Yet who claims coming destitution!

I'm surely the unluckiest waiter:
Waiting for that Waiter "round later"!

Introduction to Poem Number Forty-Eight

Withernsea – almost every *Town or Village – has a plot of land, maybe several plots of land, forgotten by everyone; sometimes forgotten even by the Owner(s)! And what can we do with these arid expanses? Put in a planning application? Convert to private car-parking? Occupy illegally? Use for outdoor rummage sales? Or develop in some other way: maybe develop in such a way, fierce controversy attracting?*

****

FORTY-EIGHT) **UNDERSTANDING THE PLOT**

There is a Plot of land
Not a big Plot of land
Within one Seaside Resort
But not quite in the middle
Of that Seaside Resort:
More towards the boundary
Of that Seaside Resort.

I do not know the *origin* of this Plot of land
Only that once it
Must have been quite an important Plot of land
Because, unusually, it is already tarmacced:
Not perfectly tarmacced
Its tarmac partially rutted and slightly fractured
But good enough hard standing:
As demanded each MidSummer
When this Plot of land is needed by caravanners:
Cravanners only caravanning
Until September 1st.

Nor do I know the *owner* of this Plot of land:
He or she who maybe purchased this Plot of land
Or inherited this Plot of land
In order to build houses on this Plot of land?
Leading he or she to fence off this Plot of land
With fencing not of good quality
But fencing of quality enough
As it sways to and fro

To reserve this Plot of land
For something else, somehow, sometime?

I only know
As just one or two skateboarders know
That this is a Plot of land
Where skateboarders can go
Until they are told not to.

Introduction to Poem Number Forty-Nine

In General Election week, 2024, I wanted to stay relevant yet not let my Verse that week stray into any field overtly party-political. So I attempted something more playful. All that held me back was finding out what to call each candidate's young ones!

****

FORTY-NINE) **CASTING THEIR VOTE?**

And in the Seaside Election
Three Candidates stand for selection:
The Dolphin, the Porpoise, the Seal....
A Contest their plans to reveal?

For the Seal, the issue is fish:
Fish quotas, fish stocks, fishmeal.

Seal pups need whole shoals to consume -
Seas free of sewage presumed?

For the Dolphin the issue is *Power:*
Turbines and Platforms; peak hours;
Expanding the North Sea's oil-field;
More pylons conveying the yield?

For the Porpoise the issue's Mobility:
Trains, buses, befitting nobility;
A Pod, Herd, or School's free passage;
No Calves, Dads or Uncles off-message?

So which of these three is a Winner?
Who promises the plentiest Dinner?
All three now parading off-shore:
First choices, high turnout, assured?

<u>Introduction to Poem Number Fifty</u>

And when the General Election was done; the Polling Stations shut; the votes all counted; canvassers sent home: many people were left in limbo, effectively redundant. That feeling of anomie affects those out-of-a-job, recently left home, moving house, unlucky following a session gambling where Loss is the only outcome.

****

FIFTY) **CONSOLATION**

There was a win
And there was a winner
Only it was someone, some ones,
Else.

There will be wins
And we will see winners
Only they will be sometime, somewhere,
Different.

There are good people
Many good people
Only they will appear, re-appear,
Later.

There will be highlights
Astonishing highlights
Outshining lowlights, very lowlights,
Earlier.

And aspiration, ambition,
Anticipation, accomplishment,
Survive untarnished, unimpeded,
Always.

<u>Introduction to Poem Number Fifty-One</u>

Withernsea has six big Public Houses on or just off its main thoroughfare Queen Street. And five of these Inns are on one side of the road, not the other....

And because one famous Missionary overseas inspired a 1958 Film: " The Inn of the Sixth Happiness," I jumped sideways here to imagine Withernsea's five Inns bringing immense happiness to both their regulars and holidaymakers passing.

****

FIFTY-ONE) **FIVE INNS of the SIXTH HAPPINESS**

Leave this Resort
Towards *Sand-le-Mer,* then Roos,
And you will see Five *Inns*:
All of them on the same side of the Road
The Left:
Five Inns of the Sixth Happiness.
And then when you leave *Sand-le-Mer*
For the Resort:
Those same Inns Five
Are still on the same side of the Road:
This time the Right
All right......*or are they*?

Because some will have Kitchens-
And some will have no Kitchen.
But surely every Inn has to have a Kitchen
To wash their glasses in? Not always *to cook* in?

So some of our Five Inns of the Sixth Happiness
Will have on their Bars
Seven Pickled Eggs or Eight bags of Prawn Crackers
Nine *Penguins* or ten *Picnic* Bars
For picnicking indoors.

And some of our Five Inns of the Sixth Happiness
Will offer live music:
Trios, Quartets , Quintets,
Cellists, Trumpeters, Guitarists, Singer-Songwriters,
Quiet dance-floors, noisier Karaoke
To nurture the next Generation
Of pavement Pavarottis.

And some of our Five Inns of the Sixth Happiness
Will offer a selection of
Slot Machines and One-Armed Bandits;
Fruit Machines where fruits must be aligned
Yielding prizes of five pounds, fifteen, *twenty-five*;
The Bingo-Caller in the background
Thankfully offering forfeited full-houses
Prizes of six pounds, sixteen, *twenty-six*.

That's if you can tear yourself away from free SKY:
The Sixth Happiness covering the sixth hole
Of the British Open;
The sixth lap of the Silverstone's Grand-Prix;
Day six of Wimbledon;
England six-nil down in Dortmund?

And when you leave one of
These Five Inns of the Sixth Happiness, *any one*,
You might have had your fill of the emptiness
Which these Five Inns were intending to fill:
Real Ale, Coates' Cider, Perry, Sherry,
Red Wine, White Wine, Vodka, Whisky, Soda...
Or: you might never leave one of these Five Inns?
But stay overnight : in Room Number Nine.

Introduction to Poem Number Fifty-Two

People who live in a Seaside Resort, full-time, can often feel isolated from the outside world; with not a lot to look forward to. In that context, big events like Carnival, the Blue Light Festival, the Switching-on of the Lights, Remembrance Sunday, providing both clear goals and wonderful memories.

Withernsea rarely charges admission, almost never a charge out-of-doors. The annual Music Festival: <<Withstock>> still goes from strength to strength, sited at the Arena in Valley Gardens.

****

FIFTY-TWO) **AND DIDN'T THEY DO WELL ?**

And as the great crowd disperses
Disappearing South North and West -
Two thousand souls and more -
An air of contentment lingers

In the warm evening air
And surely will linger longer
Beyond the late hour
When those dread words
"It is finished"
Diminish not
Excited expectation that
Just twelve months hence
Withstock will be reconvened
Restaged
....
For Withernsea's stage is now empty
Each last song sung
Each last dance danced
Each last cheer cheered
Each last drum drummed
Each last sounds sounded
Each last flame flamed
Each last wave waved
With each retarded firework
Extinguished in the darkened sky
....
And didn't they do well?
Bands so animated so enthused
They gave of heart and soul
And didn't those sellers sell well?
Sellers of blue berries
Loganberries whortleberries
Sellers of coffee and toffee
Sellers of sun hats and sombreros
Collectors of rubbish discarded
Collectors of all the loose change
Regarded as worth every penny

For the free entertainment
Of so many

Introduction to Poem Number Fifty-Three

This Poem continues the theme of Free Entertainment: what happens when a Festival is over? Particularly a very successful Festival bringing the whole Town together in glorious weather. Incidentally leaving behind a flag on every lamp-post.

****

FIFTY-THREE) **FLUTTERING**

Forty flags identical
Flying from forty identical lamp-posts
All the way along four Promenades
South to North
North to South.
Forty flags fluttering identically
In a sightly brisk South-Easterly breeze
That breeze mitigating a very hot Sunday
A very exciting Sunday
One of joy and anticipation
Maybe the joy of anticipation
Clear blue skies above
Cool blue waves below.

....

I do not know whether
A flutter is identical to a wave
Or whether those forty flags
Flutter during the night before
The day of the Event they flag up
Nor do I know whether
Those same identical flags
Flying from forty identical lamp-posts
Flutter in concert with
The nerves of those in charge of the Event
Those whose displays
Will define that Event forever
Or those whose performances
Will be remembered forever
The nerves of dozens of Event volunteers
The nerves of hundreds of Event attendees?

....

Nor do I know whether
When those forty fluttering flags
Are unpacked by different volunteers
Four days and nights before
An identical Event
But in a different year
Different people's nerves will flutter
Anticipating their different displays
Their different performances
Before different attendees
Fluttering different amounts of cash
But on identical food and drink
Playing for different prizes
But at identical booths
In different weather?

....

Good vibrations
Fluttering above
The same four beaches
Different beach boys
Playing below.

Introduction to Poem Number Fifty-Four

This Poem almost wrote itself. Inspiration came on a Saturday Morning in Midsummer when I passed a usually bustling Supermarket at 7am – crucially on the right side of the road and from the top deck of a double-decker Bus heading for Hull.

****

FIFTY-FOUR) **HOW STILL WE SEE THEE LIE**

As the Sun rises to the East
Myself heading West
From the upper deck of a Bus
I peer down on a Superstore
Slumbering before a busy Saturday ahead
Its myriad white lines as pristine
As the day white-lining first took place
With exactitude
At first cautiously, then empatically
Marking the spot
And how still I see this Emporium lie!

....

One or two of the most central bays
Will experience constant activity today
Much dropping off and picking up
While just a fraction distant
Lie a dozen or more invalidity bays
Reserved for those whose hoists will lift
Heavy tricycles or mobility scooters
Or for those who will stagger as far
As the tobacco counter
Aided by walking-stick or crow's foot
There to rest their weight
On four very different, much smaller, wheels.

....

Yet other wider, whiter bays
Are dedicated to mothers-and-toddlers
Each toddler carted, transported
In a specially adapted trolley
Young children desperate for sweets and ices
Rewarded with the aubergine, swede,
Onion and carrot that suffices
For tonight's stew
And how those busy mothers-with-toddlers
Will wish they had left
Their moaning, cantankerous, offspring
With Dad on settee staring at Donald Duck.

....

Other, narrower, white-lined bays
Are devoted to ordinary motorcars
S.U.V.s, shooting-brakes
Transporting dozens of ordinary shoppers
To their Weekend Valhalla
Their boots soon to be weighed down
With a week's worth of groceries.

Meanwhile later Bus passengers
Will look down on that first Checkout Girl
Dropped off by willing parent
Ahead of a far less willing Manageress
Soon to take charge of operations.....

Introduction to Poem Number Fifty-Five

Another Poem which almost wrote itself: the product of visiting two contrasting Seaside Fairgrounds: one Withernsea's own. And what joy and anticipation could be seen on the faces of young participants with a few pennies in their pockets.

****

FIFTY-FIVE) **HEIGH-HO! COME TO THE FAIR!**

Idlers - or mere Spectators
People passing by simply rubbernecking
But Teens with time to spare
And money to spend
Serious money exchanged
For multiple tokens purchased
Excited Teens
Come coming to the Fair
....
First the Side-shows
The hall of mirrors
Catching a duck on a stick
Throwing a sponge brick
At wobbling coconuts
Or gripping a power hose

To unseat hardboard firemen
Later shooting shot
At cardboard servicemen
Or visiting the Haunted House
Refreshed with fizzy and
Enough floss to make you dizzy
Handed out from Trailers
Their side windows unhinged
....
Then the Rides
The white-knuckle Rides
Free Fall and Flying Scooter
Hyperia and Hurricane
The Sizzler and the Swarm
Dodgems and the Dragon's Fury
Tea-Cups and Tornado
Whirligig and Wicker Man
Together with the famous Waltzer and
Whatever Carousel
Is orbiting somewhere over there
....
But wait!
Wait for the scariest Ride of all
The Ride all terrified Teens have trembled for
But none have harnessed once accessed
The dreaded Crazy Bull
The Bull that heaves each screeching Rider
Backwards, forwards, downwards, sideways
Until - no surprise - that Rider is unseated
Without majesty unseated in front of
A crowd of curious Onlookers
Only there to look onward and upward
Their free entertainment

Introduction to Poem Number Fifty-Six

At the time I wrote & submitted this Poem, Daily Newspapers or more accurately, newspapers daily, were incredibly important. They existed – no longer flourishing – to set the social and political agenda for the whole day.

But soon – very soon! – younger people will get most of their news & views from Social Media, or at least, from electronic newspapers. Leaving news-boys and news-girls redundant; newsagents struggling to find an alternative income stream: bill-paying and the National Lottery insufficient as a means of staying open.

****

FIFTY-SIX) **THE DELIVERERS**

The Courier and the Statesman
The Herald and the Scotsman
The Daily Argus and the Daily Record
The Evening Post and the Evening Standard
The Times and the Sunday Times
The Chronicle and the Good Housekeeper
The Observer and the Spectator
The Star and the Sun
All needing counting-up
And accounting for
Ready for prompt despatch
Including the Daily Despatch
………………………………………………

Thus it is a clutch of Newsboys
Plus Newsgirls such as Nell
Need recruiting
And a wake-up bell
Reveille
Rounding-up and kitting out
Including wages
Paid for the ages
They have to spend delivering
Once the white van arrives
Delivering unto them their loads
Long before the School-day begins
Their Careers ending early
Should their Papers be dumped
Somewhere unseen and unread
....

But what of their Masters?
Mistresses too
Overcome with Distress
When no Papers arrive
Or arrive too late to be read early?
Agents teetering on the edge of collapse
Unseen perhaps behind piles of News elapsed
Their businesses too about to collapse
But for the sale of chocolates and crisps
To Scholars and Friends
When the School-day ends
And what a message that sends
To followers in their footsteps
Content to get the News they follow
The Titbits they swallow
Elsewhere

Introduction to Poem Number Fifty-Seven

Like so much of my Verse: I have seen something in real life that has either enlightened or disturbed me: in this case definitely the former!

I love real life that's totally unrehearsed – at least by myself: an episode I have come across totally by chance; by being in the right place at the wrong time, or the wrong place at the right time. Serendipity.

****

FIFTY-SEVEN) **T H E   R E S C U E**

The fallen one
He who fell not in a World War
Nor from the heights of a Roof repaired
Nor down a flight of stone stairs steep
Nor - Heaven Forbid! -
From Walkways of the Humber Bridge

....

Yet he fell, intentionally fell? -
Through the jagged rocks
Norwegian rocks shipped in
To protect Withernsea's Promenade
From a North Sea on the Rampage
But who would get this man out?
On cue out came eight or nine
Volunteers of the Coastguard
To hoist him out before
A North Sea on the Rampage
Got there first to drown him

Location, location: time the essence
And Teamwork, the practised Teamwork
That might hoist him out
A man so injured so afraid
He might not be able to co-operate
In his own Survival?
Survival imperilled by circumstance

Introduction to Poem Number Fifty-Eight

Another Story – true, but anonymized – engendering anger: anger that this hobby, this crime, exists at all. Usually with no recourse to justice - or retrieval – *whatsoever. A difficult topic to cover circumspectly?*

****

FIFTY-EIGHT) **THE BICYCLE THIEF**

Raleigh around
To witness the grief caused by a Thief:
The Story of Filbert, Bike Thief-in-Chief.
But fear not Filbert, bairns so tiny...
He seeketh not your pink wheels shiny.
And fear not Filbert: dawn's News Boys:
He seeks not Bikes by no means toys.
He will not raid your Shop's outside -
To steal your livelihood and pride.
And fear not Filbert ye Bike seller:
His custom's not: "What a nice fella!"
And fear not Filbert when out riding:
He's not the Drunk with you colliding.

And fear not Filbert: your Bikes in shed;
He creeps not while you're in your bed.
And fear not Filbert: stole Bikes on E-bay:
He'll go to Market on a latter day.
No!
The Filbert to fear makes a different decision,
Out in the darkness: on deadlier Mission.
This is the Filbert with a Hammer:
So soon after exit from the Slammer.
This is the Filbert who hates ALL owners:
Insured or not, on their Shaking-boners.
This is the Filbert ignoring theft measures,
Who smashes up Bikes for curious pleasure.

ΩΩΩΩΩΩΩΩΩΩΩΩΩΩΩΩ

Introduction to Poem Number Fifty-Nine

One morning I was walking on the edge of Town when I came across a registered Cycle Proficiency Course. And the beauty of such non-statutory courses is that they take a hazardous hobby by the scruff of its neck and attempt to make it less hazardous.

Yet there are still thousands of young lads – lads more than girls – who see the pedal-bike as a toy, a toy to show-off, *rather than a serious, indeed increasingly mainstream, form of road transport.*

****

FIFTY-NINE) **TWO WHEELS: What for?**

The Scene is set
On a remote corner
Of a remote Estate
Somewhere out of Withernsea
And gathered there so many
Hi-vis tabards I have lost count
Yet each gaily clad boy
A couple of helmeted girls too
Lines up beside slumped Bicycles
Their own Bicycles indeed
They want to ride "more safer"
....
And one gaily clad Instructress
Summons a second hi-vis Instructress
To ensure this quiet road
In fact this quiet T-junction
Is completely free of Traffic
So each young participant
Can wobble along
Each on his or her wobbly machine
With due regard to
Traffic that isn't coming
....
"Look behind you!"
"Look in front of you!"
"Don't be afraid to swing your outstretched
Arm when going Right or Left"
"But don't go yet to Left or Right
In case stray Traffic should head
This way or that

Where you should have Priority"
"Now our Priority is your lifting
Each Bicycle out of the gutter
Progressing then in an orderly line
Straight back to the School Canteen"

Introduction to Poem Number Sixty

This very short Poem is in fact a Limerick. And there is no ceiling to the number of stanzas a Limerick can contain. The average Limerick length is between 1 & 4 stanzas, 13 the longest if you go on to a typical search engine.

Limericks do not have to start with the words: " There once was..." – but both the advantage and the drawback *of the Limerick is its strict form: 5 lines only, lines 1,2, and 5 rhyming; lines 3 and 4 also rhyming.*

****

SIXTY) **THE UNHAPPY INFANT**

Observe that Unhappy Child
She neither meek - nor mild
Screaming full pitch
My Studies to ditch?
Bus travel sure defiled

....

Give sop to that Screeching Child
Kiss , toy - or biscuits piled?

To buy a fragile Peace
Before bawling does increase
Would a Tigress be less wild?

Introduction to Poem Number Sixty-One

This Poem is unusual in that it isn't about anything concrete – rather the absence of anything to see here. But here is illustration of a truth known also to Teachers, Preachers and Novelists: sometimes the best source material is in front of us! It is then up to the observer to work out a way of translating one person's observation into another person's essential reading.

****

SIXTY-ONE) **THE PICTURE NONE COULD SEE?**

On the day of my departure
I noticed it
For the first time - but
Not on the first evening
Of a two-night stay
In the confines of
That room so neat
Nor at any time in between
For there was really
Nothing to notice
....

And there it was
A Frame without a Picture
Nothing fancy
For it was not a place of fancy
Two feet wide
Three foot deep
And glazed in preparation
For what? I could not conclude
My conclusion simply
Here was a Frame
Deserving some Picture
....

Had there once been a Picture
Removed at some Guest's request?
That image,
Too old? Too cold? Too bold?
Or had this room's owner
Sought to own a Picture
One day to fit that empty Frame?
Or was that emptiness
Due to be filled with an advert
Advertizing some local attraction
Cinema? Circus? Stately Home?
Distraction
....

One vision will assuredly
Accompany me here onward
There onward
How I would fill that Frame
A Frame with Picture none could see?
For I would straightway seize

One sleek horse to please?
Bleak Cartoon to tease?
Meekest Text for ease?
Something, anything
Two feet wide
Three foot deep

Introduction to Poem Number Sixty-Two

Sometimes the title of a Poem has two interpretations, or two question-marks. As with another of my real-life Poems about Rough Sleeping. Who exactly is bewildered? Maybe many more than the observer and the observed? Such is the ebb.

****

SIXTY-TWO) **BEWILDERED**

Awaiting the arrival of
The late-evening Number 75 to Withernsea
Affords me much time to
Observe my vast surroundings
Forty neatly cantilevered Bus Bays
Plus one broad concourse leading to
Seven now obscured Platforms
For Railway Trains
....
For anybody homeless
And there are many somebodies homeless
It is complex

Because this whole complex
Forbids begging
Indeed greatly restricts
Charities also begging
For loose change
Lest queueing Customers
Already uncomfortable
In relatively uncomfortable surroundings
Be further discomfited
....
And lest they be arrested
Or warned sternly to move on
To move back to the great outdoors
Adults without home must imitate passengers
Which is rather difficult
When you have not washed or eaten
For days without count
In that great outdoors now beckoning
Or should your bedraggled blanket
For that night's shop porchway
Be draped around your neck
....
Better it would be were there
A heated Waiting Room
But that is locked to, awaiting renovation
Its Sister heated Waiting Room
Seated tantalizingly
The other side of harsh ticket barriers
Even the Station's unheated Portaloo
Orphaned itself in the great outdoors beyond
Nothing for they with no home to go to
But the drain that further drains their hopes
....

Penny for the guy
The scantily-clad guy
Who three hours earlier much bewildered
Had mingled uneasily with crowds
Exiting the fabulously wealthy
Indoor Shopping Centre
Situated without congruity right next door?
That set of glass doors
Also locked against anybody
Not heading home this evening
Because home belonged if it ever did belong
Only to childhood

ΩΩΩΩΩΩΩΩΩΩΩΩΩΩΩΩΩ

Introduction to Poem Number Sixty-Three

As a student, and regular user, of Buses and Bus journeys, I'm occasionally frustrated by how not every destination panel tells me what I need to know: an expected route or reason that route is unachievable. Yet other Buses give me *almost* too much *information, such as* "Follow Us On Facebook..."

Nor has anybody – or any Company – refined their offering enough to be seen from a distance!

****

SIXTY-THREE)
WHEREVER YOU'RE HEADING THIS DAY?

I'd always understood the Double-decker Bus
Driving towards me in Hull's Prospect Street
S.N.I.S : Sorry Not in Service
Or in an even bigger City
R.T.D. : Returning to Depot
But only Overseas the Information
T.D.R. : The Driver is Resting

....

Yet by way of contrast
Long-Distance *Motor Coaches*
Do not know quite where they're going to
On the forecourt of any Motorway Service Station
You will see these shoe-box-like Vehicles
With half a sheet of copy-paper
Sellotaped to their front windscreens:
Llandudno, Llangollen, Llanberis
Brighton, Barry Island, Bridgend
Or some remote Loch or Glen
Somewhere beyond Gretna Green
In the Lowlands - or Highlands - of Scotland

....

But the future is looking much brighter
For travellers travelling towards that future
Now told so much more by those
Destination Boards displayed front or back
On their most modern Double-decker Buses
These employing thousands of yellow pixels
Scrolling down to tell you in proud affirmation
<<Merry Christmas! Happy New Year!>>

<<We Welcome Prams and Baby Buggies>>
Or *<<We Are Available.....*
To Guide Dogs? Pedal Bikes? Mobility Scooters?
<<Our Conductor is Not On Strike to-day>>
But *<<A Very Limited Timetable is in Operation*
Due to the Fog? or Snow?
That will actually *prevent* your seeing our approach!

Introduction to Poem Number Sixty-Four

What is it like to be followed? This an ever-present awareness for anybody regularly – or occasionally - *using dark or remote passageways, even well-lit Promenades.*

Being followed is most times benign. Very few people are stalked, though those who are stalked are ever on their guard. All their goings-out or comings-in complex. More common is accidental, incidental, treading up behind.

****

SIXTY-FOUR) **FOLLOW! FOLLOW! WHO WILL FOLLOW ME?**

Followed, followed: who is following me?
Yet followed, followed
I daren't turn round to see
Yet imagining it not
There seems to be
Somebody yet invisible following me

And at exactly the same pace
As if it is a race
Where he or she cannot keep up with me
But wants to?

....

And now at a glance
Or rather deprived of that rearward glance
I see no romance
In the notion somebody
Somebody whose step imitates dance
Wishes to share my journey
Join my journey indeed?
Vicariously

....

My follower is more usually accidental
Somebody who just happened
To leave his or her Gate
A second - or three - after my passing it?
Somebody deciding on Left not Right
To pursue their end
Or mine?

....

And if there is malice
Malice aforethought
In his or her stepping up to the tracking
In this quiet Town less fear of attacking?
I shall ride it out, outrun it?
For it is my fault I'm in this position
My stupidity risking another's cupidity?
My fault that momentarily distracted
I attracted such a following?

Introduction to Poem Number Sixty-Five

Sometimes a small Town is treated to an event completely different from any other. Such was the outdoor Nativity before Christmas 2024: a Pageant loosely based on both Sheffield and Oberammergau's Passion plays. Again I was fortunate that this Poem could be composed and printed in just one week.

****

SIXTY-FIVE) : **NOUGHT FOR THEIR COMFORT?**

Take a lonely donkey
Five Sheep - and a recent Calf
Add three prancing Horses
Three steadfast Steeds trialled for Dressage
To meet our Producer's quite extraordinary needs
Together with a cherubic new-born Baby
A really doting Mother
An authentically affectionate Father
Two surreal Angels
Stir briskly this diverse mixture
And you have our evolving Nativity
Moreover our *revolving* Nativity
Out-of-doors
....
Nor is this Scene-setting, this Wintry Scenery
This Pageant outwith
Reassuring Doors
Free of risk
The risk certain Shepherds and Kings

Will go AWOL or go out on strike that day ?
The risk Babe or Beast
Will require a nappy-change?
The risk an unhappy Participant
Will decide he or she is needed elsewhere?
The risk the Microphones, the technology
Will not hum, will not come, on the Night?
Or the risk somebody central will go off-message?
Hazards demanding Attendants in hi-vis jackets

....

And didn't they do well?
Attracting to the stage of Valley Gardens
A devoted, devotional, Crowd
Larger than any but that ten years ago to hear
The Arch-bishop of York preaching, teaching:
Their talk, their carolling, their sense of belonging
Clerical, unhysterical - *and enquiring*
Their attention, their attentiveness, requiring
Good weather whether or not
That benevolence will travel over the Ocean
In time to counter the notion
That this Seaside Resort
Has shuttered up while Easter?

Introduction to Poem Number Sixty-Six

Unconsciously, as I'm walking, I'm noticing the rear number-plates of mainly cars. Because cars when they're parked-up are really metal sculptures: not actually doing *anything.*

And again without much attention, I'm noticing cherished number-plates above others: which might be why some car-owners purchase them?

****

SIXTY-SIX) **CHERISH THE THOUGHT**

Bev and Kev
Ben and Ken
And any number for folk whose
Names rhyme with "ill"
Bill and Jill
Till and Hill
For this is the incentive to purchase
A *Cherished* Number Plate
Sometimes called a Personalized Number Plate
Sometimes a Custom or Prestige Number Plate
Anything to distinguish that person's car
From the Vehicle belonging to their Neighbour
....

So are these very special Number Plates common?
Common although they aim to be *Uncommon*?
Common because some people have money to spare
A lot of money
Less money
If they are ready to travel to the Town
Identified by the prefix or suffix
They seek to cherish
Perish the thought
....

And do passers-by notice the Cherished Number Plate?
The answer: Passers-by *do indeed* notice
Or else nobody would go to all the trouble
Of sourcing GDP1 or AGD2
While assuredly rejecting FGM3 and POM4
The trials of transferring
Two fragile rectangles of acrylic
From some old banger gracing someone else's Drive
Onto the brand new Sports' Utility Vehicle
Heralded to arrive any minute now
One Very Important Person's ingenuity
....
For it takes a great deal of ingenuity
To cloak your Number Plate in mystery
To tease sense out of
The most bizarre Registration bought from the Bazaar
Like the one that hides the name EMMA or ANDY?
ALISON or JENNY?
While saving each endowed Owner
Or each present Proprietor
Several hundred pounds
Several *thousand* pounds
The more numbers that get in the way of the letters
Or the more of those letters that need shifting, spacing
Until it all reads as you want it to read
Or will it?

ΩΩΩΩΩΩΩΩΩΩΩΩΩΩΩΩ

<u>Introduction to Poem Number Sixty-Seven</u>

One of the advantages of five-day Coach Tours is the length of time it gives each Passenger in the company of his or her Driver. They see close-hand how important is this job: a job that often includes the rôle of Courier. Can it be done?

Incidentally, how can any *Coach Driver fill "rest" hours when nothing is happening beyond parking-up?*

****

SIXTY-SEVEN) **THOSE HOURS IN BETWEEN**

There's Pete and there's Gordon
There's Greg and there's Jordan
Then there's *Me*
All five of us hired by Twix'Tween Coaches
As Summer Two-Eighteen hotly approaches
Then put out to grass - and made redundant
While cases of *Covid* are most abundant
Taken back again at the close of Two-Twenty-One
For each Excursion or Outing kept in harness
From daybreak till setting of the Sun
On minimum pay and maximum delay.
....

Only I'm not like posh Pete or dreary Gordon
Hearing Greg - or seeing Jordan
Because I occupy my steering days out and about
Dreary hours no doubt

Weary hours no doubt
From dropping-off Customers
To picking those same Customers up again
For some jollity halting at *frivolity*.
....

Not for me slipping away alongside other Drivers
For chatter or Poker at Noon
Not for me nipping off to bet on the gee-gees
Or sipping Tea in some Greasy-Spoon
Not for me kipping on my Bus's back seat
Or getting to grips: some knotty Crossword to complete
More my going for dips in the English Channel
Or closing the Lock-gates of our trip's Canal
Boarding a pleasure-ship to the next Bay
In each Minster's Chancel: a rare chance to pray.
....

Or
Disadvantaged while sharing my Coach-load's Band
I slink away with an hour in hand
And on their Tour of a Stately Hall
I tell the Guide I must answer a call
And soon after munching my packed lunch
I quit the Boxing Ring past the ninth punch
At Royal Worcester I soak up their history
But leave before solving *a Murder Mystery*
In truth I am doing what my Parties do
Using as they do the Visitors' Loo
I delight in whatever my Colleagues are ignoring
Back at the Yard appealing, imploring
For rather more than the Minimum Wage.

ΩΩΩΩΩΩΩΩΩΩΩΩΩΩΩΩΩΩ

Introduction to Poem Number Sixty-Eight

In this Poem I return to that troubling Subject of Homelessness. I was in Paris when I learnt how a carefully shelved shop-frontage can provide greater "comfort" for someone dispossessed than bare tarmac. Different design slightly – maybe only slightly? - addressing a very troubled scene of total hopelessness.

****

SIXTY-EIGHT) **O N T H E S H E L F**

Not every shopping street has one
A Shop with a Shelf
A broad and rounded ledge
In front of plate-glass window inset:
So kind to a Sleeper's health?

....

For Sleepers left on the Shelf
Though not in the best of health
Love that Shelf enough
To leave a damp sleeping-bag
And a blanket or two
On the Shelf
A sign of their wealth?
Till later that same day

....

But how do these Sleepers sleep
Through the chatter of Pubs turning out?
Through the loud churning of traffic?
And terrific clatter
Of the early-morning road-sweeper?
....
Maybe these rough Sleepers
These admirably tough Sleepers
Get used to being left on the Shelf?
Three foot above contradiction
Three foot above the gutter ignominious
About to be swept with utter diligence?
Magnanimous heights of superiority
Till challenges of the Morrow

ΩΩΩΩΩΩΩΩΩΩΩΩΩΩΩΩΩΩ

Introduction to Poem Number Sixty-Nine

Only by the Seaside is it relatively common to find one person who creates a whole Town set out to the specifications of that one man's vision. But that is true of Fleetwood, Saltburn and Llandudno along with Withernsea: the Lord Mayor of Hull, Anthony Bannister's new watering place.

****

SIXTY-NINE) :
ONE BANNISTER , MANY BALUSTERS

" You've heard of this thing called RAIL:
I doubt that it can fail
A New Line is my boast
A line to the Yorkshire *Coast*
There is this little Village
Known past for smuggling, pillage
But so promising its Beach
Which this New Line will reach!

....

" Promising too its fine Sea air
All maladies to repair
Promising its fishing ground
Where dabs, whiting, cod abound
Crabs and Lobsters fine
For Cities where rich folk do dine!
Miles enough for a Prom
Where Minstrels can go pom-pom-pom!

....

" A Lighthouse shall we build
Lest Sailors tossed be killed
A Gas Board shall we raise
Four Churches God to praise
A Pier a third-of-a-mile long
Its Stanchions broad and strong
A Station oh so pleasant
For Duchess or for Peasant!

....

" Our Hotel we'll call "Queen's"
For folk of ample means
And Cyclists by the Million
Will find a "Grand Pavilion...."
And those not confident Sailors
Will fear not Boating Lake failure
In all a Resort of *worth*
A Brighton of the North

ΩΩΩΩΩΩΩΩΩΩΩΩΩΩΩΩΩΩΩ

Introduction to Poem Number Seventy

The advantage of a weekly local newspaper that it can touch on the very topical. So it was: with the recent and emotional 60th. Anniversary of Richard Beeching's withdrawal of Withernsea's Railway.

Not just any old trains derailed - but an entire Seaside Resort's future and prosperity: this Town so dependent on a direct link with its nearest City. The slow Bus alternative never really worked - despite a cohort of wonderful Drivers.

****

SEVENTY) **THE TRAIN NOW DEPARTING**

The Train now departing Platform One
Will not be stopping here
Ever

....

The Train now gliding past Platform Two
Will be returning
Never

....

Carriages to Hull and back
Ran on time whate'er the
Weather

....

You tried too late to keep your Route
A magnificent
Endeavour

....

Our manoeuvring to cut you off
Was false accounting
Clever

....

In months to come
The track we'll lift
Then sever

....

Future Commuters on their Bus
Will reach the end of their
Tether

.... As Golden Hordes of Trippers glad
Absent themselves
Forever